"Sue Hershkowitz-Coore i___ ... munication techniques. B___ for sales professionals and ___ ess guide for everyone who r___ ua- sive communication are the ___ hat the field of specialization. As a strategist, my best advice is to buy it, learn it, implement it . . . before your competition does, and you're left with no advantages other than your looks and dumb luck!"

—David Rich, Senior Vice President, Strategic Marketing/
Worldwide, George P. Johnson Experience Marketing

"Sue's uplifting positive energy and easy, practical advice shine through on every page. She marries sound selling strategy with foolproof tactics, so you really can't go wrong. It's like having your own sales coach. Put Sue's principles into practice and you'll feel better about yourself—and you'll do better, too."

—Raymond Stevens, Director, Staples University, Staples, Inc.

"This practical little book covers it all: important communication and telephone, writing, and presentation skills for sales success! You'll build stronger relationships when you apply the key words and strategies Sue provides."

—Scott Russell, Vice President, International Sales Office,
The Ritz-Carlton Hotel Company

"A wonderful and practical reference tool to keep in your back pocket. Sue Hershkowitz-Coore has filled every page with nuts and bolts advice. You need this book!"

—Louis Beck, Chairman of the Board of U.S. Bancorp of
Ohio/CEO and Chairman/CEO of Janus Hotels and Resorts

"Sue Hershkowitz-Coore is the 'Queen of Communication,' but now she has outdone herself. As a salesperson you will no longer have to worry about what to say or write. Sue supplies you with the perfect words or phrases for every situation: even the ones you'd rather avoid. I've been in sales for thirty-five years and I have prof- ited from this book. You will, too."

—Warren Greshes, author of *The Best Damn Sales Book Ever*

"A great read for anyone who wants to improve their sales. This in- sightful book gives sales managers practical information that they can use immediately. These commonsense ideas are easy to under- stand and will make you a better salesperson."

—Fred Shea, Vice President Sales, Hyatt Hotels Corporation

continued . . .

"*How to Say It to Sell It* is filled with hundreds of specific, real-world selling tips to help you talk, write, and present a sales message that wins the business. Turn to any page and learn something valuable."

—Howard Putnam, former CEO of Southwest Airlines,
author of *The Winds of Turbulence*

"Words truly matter . . . *How to Say It to Sell It* clearly shows you how to boost sales, close deals, increase revenue, and guarantee success by choosing the right words and delivering them in a way that makes the difference. It's brilliantly simple, extremely practical, and delightfully written . . . essential reading for sales winners!"

—Roger Dow, President/CEO, Travel Industry Association,
former Marriott SVP of Global Sales

"Words and how you use them are powerful tools for the successful salesperson. *How to Say It to Sell It* is packed with nuggets that will help you communicate better to make more sales. Your competitors might use the right words but this book will show you how to use the best words."

—Mark Sanborn, author of *The Fred Factor* and
You Don't Need a Title to Be a Leader

"*The* critical guide to improving your persuasive selling language that needs to be in every sales professional's back pocket. Applying these ideas *will* increase your selling success!"

—Jim Pancero, author of *You Can Always Sell More*

"Sue Hershkowitz-Coore's new book is packed with pragmatic ways to sell your ideas, products, and anything else that matters. Instead of wasting your valuable time on platitudes or abstract theories, she provides real-life suggestions you'll be able to use immediately. Read it and reap."

—Sam Horn, fifteen-time emcee of the Maui Writers
Conference, author of *POP!*

"In today's fast-paced business environment you don't have the luxury of time to remake a first impression. *How to Say It to Sell It* offers countless practical and helpful hints . . . written in a fun, entertaining style . . . a must-read for anyone looking to win business and enhance relationships."

—Richard B. Green, Vice President, Association Business Development and Strategic Partnerships, Marriott International

"Sales process tells salespeople what to do and Sue's book tells how to do it!"

—Brian J. Dietmeyer, President/CEO, Think! Inc.

HOW TO SAY IT TO SELL IT

*Key Words, Phrases, and Strategies
to Build Relationships, Boost Revenue,
and Beat the Competition*

Sue Hershkowitz-Coore

PRENTICE HALL PRESS

PRENTICE HALL PRESS
Published by the Penguin Group
Penguin Group (USA) Inc.
375 Hudson Street, New York, New York 10014, USA
Penguin Group (Canada), 90 Eglinton Avenue East, Suite 700, Toronto, Ontario M4P 2Y3, Canada
(a division of Pearson Penguin Canada Inc.)
Penguin Books Ltd., 80 Strand, London WC2R 0RL, England
Penguin Group Ireland, 25 St. Stephen's Green, Dublin 2, Ireland (a division of Penguin Books Ltd.)
Penguin Group (Australia), 250 Camberwell Road, Camberwell, Victoria 3124, Australia
(a division of Pearson Australia Group Pty. Ltd.)
Penguin Books India Pvt. Ltd., 11 Community Centre, Panchsheel Park, New Delhi—110 017, India
Penguin Group (NZ), 67 Apollo Drive, Rosedale, North Shore 0632, New Zealand
(a division of Pearson New Zealand Ltd.)
Penguin Books (South Africa) (Pty.) Ltd., 24 Sturdee Avenue, Rosebank, Johannesburg 2196,
South Africa

Penguin Books Ltd., Registered Offices: 80 Strand, London WC2R 0RL, England

While the author has made every effort to provide accurate telephone numbers and Internet addresses at the time of publication, neither the publisher nor the author assumes any responsibility for errors, or for changes that occur after publication. Further, the publisher does not have any control over and does not assume any responsibility for author or third-party websites or their content.

Copyright © 2008 by Sue Hershkowitz-Coore
Cover art by Paul Howalt
Cover design by Ben Gibson
Text design by Tiffany Estreicher

First edition: January 2008

Library of Congress Cataloging-in-Publication Data

Hershkowitz-Coore, Sue.
  How to say it to sell it : key words, phrases, and strategies to build relationships, boost revenue, and beat the competition / Sue Hershkowitz-Coore.
     p. cm.
  ISBN 978-0-7352-0426-3
  1. Selling. 2. Business communication. 3. Sales presentations. I. Title.
  HF5438.25.H475 2008
  658.85—dc22   2007041015

PRINTED IN THE UNITED STATES OF AMERICA

10 9 8 7 6 5 4 3 2

Most Prentice Hall Press books are available at special quantity discounts for bulk purchases for sales promotions, premiums, fund-raising, or educational use. Special books, or book excerpts, can also be created to fit specific needs. For details, write: Special Markets, Penguin Group (USA) Inc., 375 Hudson Street, New York, New York 10014.

To

Bill—Bashert. Love of my life. Everything is you.

Michael—Mensch. Your kind heart overwhelms me.

Mom—For offering your love always.

And to my daddy—My inspiration.

Acknowledgments

The great philosopher "Anonymous" said, "There is a lot of growing up between 'it fell' and 'I broke it.'" There's also a lot between "here's *my* book," and "here's a book that wouldn't have happened without a loving support team." So, my heartfelt gratefulness to my husband, Bill, for his constant love and gentle spirit; my son, Michael; and mother, Lois, for your love and patience.

Thank you to Nance Wickins, Lily Henson, Josie Varga, and Patrick Rhone—my A team. Thank you, Joe Charbonneau, my mentor; Brian Kennedy, an American hero; and my daddy, who, again, would have liked this idea.

Thank you to all my workshop attendees, to all my clients, and to all my "SpeakerSue" fans. You challenge me to teach precise, practical, and immediately usable sales advice—and this book is a reflection of that.

Finally, thank you to Barry Neville, Joan Matthews, and my editor, Maria Gagliano. Thank you, Maria, for not letting me use the first draft.

CONTENTS

Introduction

This book is about standing apart from the crowd. Each page is filled with specific, easy-to-apply, practical nuggets of information to help you create the relationships and sales success that can often seem so unattainable.

Hard work, desire, and persistence alone don't make sales dreams come true. Knowing what to say and how to say it persuasively, professionally, and powerfully are key. Salespeople who sell the most communicate their message in a way that separates them from their competitive set. They build long-term profitable relationships because their communications are credible and customer-centric.

You may have heard that some people are "born" salespeople. No such thing exists. Great salespeople communicate so comfortably and competently that they appear to have a special gift. It's not a gift. It's a communication process they've perfected, most likely, over years and by trial and error. You don't have to take years to learn that communication process. This book will give you the tools you need to communicate with your clients and customers with ease and success.

Most salespeople want answers. Yet look through a dozen books on selling and what do you find? If you're lucky, you read about how someone (the writer) became successful. The challenge is that the recommended techniques are often based on that individual's style, type of prospects and customers, products, personal philosophy, faith, or closing cycles. This book isn't like that. This book answers the question: How do I say that to make the sale? It alleviates the pain of not knowing exactly what to say to invite the prospect to buy.

Books on selling strategies often focus on attitude, goal setting, and motivation. No other book focuses specifically on the critical communication aspect of selling. In this book, you'll find sample words, key phrases, and practical, real-world scripts you can tailor to communicate *your* particular sales message to *your* clients, prospects, and customers. This book isn't about motivation; it's about communicating so they remember you, like you, and want to buy from you.

You went into sales to be in control of your earning potential, to influence others, and to create success for yourself and others. The specific, easy-to-apply concepts in this book will teach you how to do that. You'll learn the communication secrets that drive revenue and build loyal relationships to propel your sales career.

This book is divided into four parts, each emphasizing a different and crucial aspect of the sales process. In these parts, you'll find two overarching points that are relevant to every sales situation:

1. **Communicate in a customer-centric manner.** When you focus on what matters to your customers rather than on what is important to you, you separate your-

self from your competition, boost sales success, and build meaningful and profitable relationships. Show people you care about their well-being, and they'll be more likely to care about what you have to say. Being customer-centric may be the most self-serving sales strategy of all. When customers and prospects know that your goal is to help them create greater success, the more successful you become.

2. **Be more persuasive and less informational.** Your website and other collateral communicate data; your job is to persuade your prospect to say "yes." The more persuasive you are, the more likely you are to capture and keep his attention. Information alone can be boring and statistics are useless facts unless your buyer understands what they mean to her. As you learn to communicate more persuasively, selling your product, service, or idea becomes easier, more profitable, and more fun.

PART I. KEYS TO SUCCESSFUL SALES CONVERSATIONS

Excellent conversational skills and strong interpersonal relationships are the primary contributors to sales success. Yet if you're like most salespeople, you've been given extensive product training and little or no communication skills training. You're expected to depend on your charm, charisma, and "natural ability" to keep the sales conversation flowing. But all the product information in the world won't help when the prospect says, "You sound just like everyone else," or "Thanks, but we're happy with our current vendor."

Acquiring the skills to handle any sales conversation professionally and persuasively is what we'll focus on throughout this book, and especially in Part I. I'll begin by revealing a little-known listening technique that will significantly boost your ability to influence the sale. You'll also learn to keep the sales conversation flowing, handle objections, and maintain control of the sale. Through scripts, specific steps, and key words, you'll learn the most productive ways to build relationships and enhance credibility in an open dialogue.

Each part and chapter of this book provides tips and ideas you can apply immediately to create meaningful sales conversations. Part I gives you the foundation you need to sell in today's marketplace. The entire book, however, helps you create and maintain persuasive and profitable sales conversations. To me, a successful sales conversation, whether you're talking face to face, presenting to 15 or 1,500 prospects, or sending a follow-up email, results in forward movement toward your desired result. *Every* communication is a conversation.

PART II. SELLING IT ON THE PHONE

Creating new opportunities and growing business are critical to sales success. But how do you engage someone over the phone when he doesn't know you? How do you spark his interest? In just a few seconds, how do you build rapport and credibility? How do you get your message across to your prospects when they won't even take your call? Most fundamental of all, how do you psych yourself up to actually make the calls? Your cold-calling approach— whether you speak to prospects directly or leave voice messages—determines whether you get the appointment and make the sale, or not.

Part II talks about the critical communication skills involved in selling to REAL prospects over the phone. You'll learn how to eliminate rejection and boost revenue by changing your cold-calling objectives. I'll show you why you need to challenge common practices and replace them with new ways to persuade prospects to take your call, respond to you, and phone you back. Step-by-step rules and scripts that you can customize for specific sales situations will help you open your call persuasively and communicate your message to get the sale in motion.

PART III. HIGH-IMPACT PRESENTATIONS THAT SELL

Have you ever thought, "I wish I had more time to prepare for this presentation"? Have you ever settled for a "good" presentation instead of one that was memorable? If so, you're like most sales professionals; you're too busy selling to take the time to create the most persuasive and compelling sales argument.

A well-prepared sales presentation serves to set you and your products apart from the competition. By structuring presentations to capture your prospects' attention from your very first words, and engaging them throughout the two-step conclusion and close, your pitches will book more business.

Part III helps you master your pitch. Whether you have five minutes or five hours, are talking to one or one hundred decision makers, you'll learn to present your message with greater confidence. You'll learn how to build rapport, establish credibility, and create memorability. You will sound better than your competition!

PART IV. SELLING IT IN WRITING

The best way to grow your business is to stay connected to your customers. But breaking through competitive clutter, particularly when it comes to email, takes more than offering a great product and great service. Even if your customers are just across town, the people competing for their attention are likely across the country or the globe. Your worldwide competition can email them exactly as you can. How do you separate yourself from the competition and persuade your prospect to open, read, and respond to your message? How do you let your customer know what's new and what's important? How do you break through the clutter to maintain relationships, build new ones, and create lasting ones?

In Part IV, we'll look at the most common email mistakes and how to avoid them when creating sales proposals and other email messages. By applying a three-step process to your writing, you'll save up to 80 percent of the time you currently spend writing, and you'll communicate your content more powerfully.

With lists of power words to use—and those to avoid that turn buyers away—you'll stand out from the crowd and enjoy new success every time you write. From showing your customers how you attend to detail to adhering to the best practices in email etiquette, you'll learn how to create sales messages that sizzle and sell. You'll never hide behind email again; instead, you'll be prepared to use your written business communication as a critical money-making sales tool.

Beating the competition today takes more than knowing the right words to use; it's about using the *best* words to build trusting relationships. It's not just about providing information or even creating value for your customer; it's about communicating that information and value in a customer-centric and persuasive manner so they get it. This book teaches you how to do that.

PART I

Keys to Successful Sales Conversations

Great sales conversations rely on a confident salesperson. Anyone can talk and many people can exude charm, but profitable sales professionals communicate at a different level. They purposefully and persuasively communicate trust and value. More than anything, they help their buyers feel safe enough to continue the sales conversation. Once a buyer feels uncomfortable in any way, he or she shuts down, shuts up, and shuts the seller out. Persuading the buyer to do anything at that point becomes almost impossible regardless of how compelling the product and sales pitch are. Both the sale and the relationship are doomed.

To make buyers feel safe and comfortable enough to talk about their needs and wants, constantly listen for points of agreement. Once you find a common ground, highlight this commonality and use words to support and affirm your client's mind-set. This is especially important in times of disagreement during a conversation. You must create an environment where the customer is comfortable explaining her buying motivations and willing to explore alternative ways to reach her goals. Part I shows you how to build rapport during a sales conversation and navigate the dialogue even when your buyer may be rude, uninterested, or complacent with her existing processes.

1

Listening to Overcome Objections

Most of the successful people I've known are the ones who do more listening than talking.
—Bernard M. Baruch

While earning my masters in counseling, I came across a listening skill that changed my life. Prior to learning it, if someone I was trying to persuade said to me, "I can't see how your idea will work," instead of listening to him, I'd do my best to show him how it *would* work. What was I doing? I was telling him he was wrong! I wasn't listening. I was being disrespectful *to my customer*.

Listening to your customer may be the hardest skill to master because salespeople like to talk. We like to talk about ourselves, our product, and our ideas. But one of the first keys to winning business is to talk less and listen more. By listening to your customers' objections and responding respectfully and earnestly to what you hear, you'll immediately create a trusting atmosphere. When you have the ability to help people—customers, clients, and prospects—feel comfortable and safe around you, you have the ability to increase your influence and win more sales.

Listening and responding to objections in a customer-centric manner is not a manipulative tool, though seeing example after example in this chapter may smack of "fake." These examples show you how this skill works in various sales settings, but try using it without authenticity, without caring about the best interests of your customer, or without believing your own words, and you won't succeed. Use these skills to show respect for your customer, and watch your sales grow.

Here is a simple, five-step process for effective listening:

Step 1. Listen for points of agreement. As your prospect speaks, maintain a steady focus on the points you have in common. Encourage him to keep talking by accepting his point of view.

Step 2. If your customer disagrees with you, don't be quick to prove him wrong. Instead, listen for his hidden question. Ask yourself: What is he really asking, and how can I show that my solution answers that question?

Step 3. Respond by talking about how you agree. Highlight what you have in common. Use words such as "You're right" or "Yes" to begin your response.

Step 4. When you can't agree, or think you can't agree, consider what the prospect is really asking. Is there a way that you can agree with anything she has said? Think about what she really wants to know. As long as she keeps talking, no matter how negative she sounds, she wants answers to, sometimes, unspoken questions.

Address her concerns by providing your solutions to the issues you hear.

Step 5. Determine the next step. Listening to a prospect's objections and comments gives you the opportunity to overcome those issues. Don't stop there. Show her how your idea, product, or service is the best solution. Then, move on to the next step: ask for the action you want.

LISTEN FOR POINTS OF AGREEMENT

Listening for points of agreement is a life skill that revolutionizes the way you communicate, persuade, and influence. It overcomes resistance. It disarms people. It moves them from closed-mindedness to open. Applying this skill turns you into a persuasive listener.

Tom Crum, a black belt in the martial art of aikido, spoke to this communication concept in his quote "Would you rather be happy or right?" We each have a choice. We can stand our ground and try to steamroll ahead with our point and be "right," or we can step back, accept the other person's viewpoint, respectfully help him move in another direction, and be "happy." When I studied aikido, I'd watch some people, seemingly effortlessly, toss "attackers" twice their size. Yet, I also watched as others struggled to move people half their size. The difference? Those who performed effortlessly and were successful in changing their attacker's minds (about fulfilling their desire to attack) stepped *back* to accept the oncoming attack. Those who couldn't budge their opponent stuck to their ground. They believed that by strong-arming their opponents, they could sell their point (don't attack me), but the attacker just kept attacking. Eventually, the people who stuck to their view would end up thrown to the mat instead of the other way around.

First, you need to openly listen. I'm not talking about simply paying attention; I'm talking about listening for the points you can agree with. To listen for points of agreement, you only need ask yourself:

- What has this person said that I can ethically agree with?
- How can I help him "be right"?

The aikido master's stepping back concept helps you listen for points of agreement. Imagine that you're in the midst of a sales pitch and your prospect interrupts you and says, "That really won't work here." Did you hear anything you might agree with? If you stand your ground and respond, "Yes, it will," you'll embolden the "opponent"—your customer—to continue his attack. Instead, listen carefully so you can help *the other person* be right.

It does seem that agreeing with her negative statement might be impossible. Step back for a moment. Is there a way that you *might* be able to affirm your prospect's thinking? Is there a way to make him right? Even if you *think* you're 100 percent correct, think about how you can align your thinking with hers. In this instance, you absolutely believe your solution *will* work perfectly for your buyer (or you wouldn't be offering it), yet can't you also authentically agree that it's possible that it *may* not work there? Could there be any situation that might exist for the buyer that could prevent your solution from working? Of course, that's possible! But it doesn't need to stop the sales conversation.

By not pushing prospects and customers to support or defend their point of view, you help them listen to yours.

LISTEN FOR THEIR HIDDEN QUESTION

When someone puts up a rigid roadblock such as "that won't work here," it can be difficult to figure out what you can ethically agree with if you don't know where to look. By listening not only to his statement, but to the question that lies behind it, you're able to address his concern and provide a solution that will move the conversation forward.

Remember she said to you: "That really won't work here."

What is she really asking? The underlying question is: How *can* it work here?

Answer her question:

YOU: What we've found is that a beta test of the software involving as few as two employees, more if you'd like, can confirm if there are cost savings *to you*.

By answering the underlying question, you confirm that you have truly listened to your buyer. In doing so, you build the relationship and enhance your trustworthiness in your buyer's eyes.

HOW TO SAY IT: USE POWER WORDS

You've probably figured out by now that the words you use to let your prospect know you heard her message, and can see her point of view, are critical to keeping the conversation going. The two most powerful words you will ever use to let anyone know she's made a valid point are: "You're right." It's plain, truthful, and clear.

Here are other power words to use to indicate you've heard their point:

Yes, and . . .

I agree, and . . .

I respect what you're saying, and . . .

I can see your point and . . .

I hear what you're saying and . . .

TALK ABOUT HOW YOU AGREE

Persuasive listening gives you the tools to overcome your customers' objections and simultaneously build rapport. Always keep the focus of the conversation on the areas of agreement rather than the points you may disagree on.

Example:

You rep office products and your goal is to persuade your customer to give you a list of the products she typically orders from her current supplier so you can provide comparison prices.

YOU: We'd like to show you how we can save you at least 15 percent off the cost of your office supplies.

PROSPECT: We have an excellent relationship with our current supplier and I see no need to compare prices.

Accept what you heard her say. Help her "be right" so she can relax and open up to the possibilities you're offering. Because the prospect has told you her truth—that she has an excellent relationship with her current supplier—you've already been given a point you can agree with. Your words must show her you've heard and respect her position. This will surprise and disarm her. Because everyone enjoys being affirmed and feeling accepted at her word, your prospect relaxes and is ready to hear what else you have to say. After accepting her truth, move on to solving her issue and answering her underlying question; she has an excellent supplier relationship so *tell her how you can make it worthwhile for her to put that relationship aside.*

> **YOU: Yes. Your relationship with your current supplier is excellent, and that is an important part of the decision. Our goal is to help you save so much money in your procurement process that you might consider beginning another great supplier relationship. Would you be comfortable allowing me to provide you with a complimentary price comparison? No strings attached, of course.**

Example:

The venture capitalist says to you, "I've been in business longer than you've been alive."

As tempted as you might be to say, "Don't worry, I can see that you're older than dirt" (which would certainly be finding a point of agreement!), you'll be much more successful if you find a truthful and *respectful* way to agree with his comment. Let him know you accept his point, and move to a solution.

> **YOU: You're right. You have been in business longer than I've been alive, and here are the three things I believe I can help you achieve . . .**

By listening for the point you can agree with, and starting your response highlighting how you agree (rather than highlighting disagreement), you diffuse his confrontational behavior. You move the sales conversation in the direction you want it to go by addressing his concerns.

Example:

Imagine that you are a sales manager for a hotel and you're five minutes into your presentation to the decision-making committee. The meeting professional leading the committee stops you and says, "You sound exactly like the other two hotel companies that spoke to us this morning. I just can't believe that no one has anything that we can get excited about."

Agree and accept what you can. Let her know you've heard her truth by addressing the objection. Rather than standing your ground and disagreeing, find a way to help her "be right." Let her know that you have solutions to offer to her insightful comment.

It *is* true that you and the other two hotel companies *might* sound similar. You both have sleeping rooms, meeting space, ballrooms, and food and beverage. She's right! You do sound alike. Tell her!

YOU: You're right. We really must sound the same. And in many ways we are. The one exciting benefit we can offer you that's exclusive to the Pups Hotel Company is . . .

HOW NOT TO SAY IT: WORDS THAT UNDERMINE LISTENING FOR AGREEMENT

Because your goal is to be a persuasive listener and show your customer that you're tuned in to what he is saying, it's important to eliminate words that present an opposite picture.

If your prospect said, "This won't work around here," and instead of finding a way to agree with what you heard him say, you counteracted his response and said, "No. It really will work here," he would disengage from the conversation. You've implied, "You're wrong and I'm right."

Here's the rub: Even if you *are* right, even if it will absolutely, positively work, it won't matter to your prospect for two reasons:

1. Once he states what he thinks, he'll do everything possible to stay consistent with that opinion.
2. Given a choice, he will buy from people he likes—people who, in his opinion, are agreeable and open-minded.

The following words contradict your customer and, without additional clarification and some tap dancing on your part, will prevent the sales conversation from moving forward.

No. (Read more about this on page 36.)
You're wrong.
I don't understand what you're saying.
That doesn't make sense.
That isn't right.
But. (Read more about this on page 40.)

WHEN YOU CAN'T AGREE, LISTEN AGAIN

Sometimes you hear nothing that you can agree with. The prospect tells you that you have the highest prices for goods, your service reputation is crummy, your delivery is slow, your location is inconvenient, and your mama is ugly. And it's all true.

When you feel like you have no option other than to defend your prices, service, or delivery process, get creative! Look for another way to sincerely answer a prospect's question and solve his problem. No problem has just one solution yet even the best of us sometimes fall into the "this will never fly" trap. Listen to the hidden question and be willing to present a new perspective, even if it isn't always to the most obvious route. It just might be the answer your prospect was looking for.

Accept his message and redirect him to yours:

Example:

Your customer says to you: "Your price is higher than your competitors." And it is. Listen persuasively. He's asking you to confirm his truth. Because your price *is* higher than your competitor's, you can easily agree with him. Affirm what you've heard and then move on to your persuasive sales message. In a case such as this one, some additional insight into how a seemingly high price could actually benefit the customer's bottom line won't be expected, but it can be just the thing to turn the conversation back around to a more promising direction.

YOU: You're right. The price appears high because the initial cost is 3 percent more. By reducing the need for replacement parts, the actual cost is 11 percent less than current product pricing. How often do you estimate that you need replacement parts for the current product? Two,

**three times a year? That's a significant overall price break
equaling a savings of over $500 for each of your twenty-
five units yearly.**

Example:

You're the sales manager for Restaurant Buster, and
you're showing a bride and her mother the space you have
available for the wedding. The bride is quite excited until
the mother says to you, "This space is too small for 300 people. We'll be way too cramped." She turns to her daughter,
"Honey, if you want to have your reception here, we have to
limit the number of guests to 250."

She's right. Stuffing that many guests into the room will
be claustrophobic. Agree with the question she's asked you
(Is this room too small for 300 guests?), and then offer your
creative solution.

**YOU: You're right. This space is too small for 300 people.
What works beautifully for that number is to extend this
room with a tent. The room can then be set so that your
guests who'd like to enjoy the wonderful dinner and quietly talk to each other while they dine can do so, and your
guests who want to be dancing and partying can have
their space, too.**

OFFER YOUR SOLUTION AND
THE NEXT STEP

Initially, your prospect objected to your value proposition.
Something didn't suit him. Because you listened persuasively, you were able to help him calm down and focus on

the solutions you had for him. Now, advance the sale by asking or confirming the next logical action.

Ask questions such as:

What's the next step?

What would you like the next step to be?

How would you like me to handle the next step?

How would you like me to follow up?

Which of these options sounds best to you?

With your approval, we could . . . Would that be okay?

Would Tuesday or Friday be more convenient for you to meet with me?

When would be the best time to follow up with you then? June? September?

These questions, unlike a "presumptive close," do not presume the buyer is buying ("How many of these shall I deliver to your home?" *or* "Will one tie be enough with this suit?"). Your goal is to make sure the conversation doesn't end without determining what your prospect would like to see as the next natural step in the process.

These additional examples demonstrate the five steps to overcoming objections:

CUSTOMER: It doesn't work that way in this industry.
YOU: You're right. It's a new practice for this industry. What we've found in industries that have been using this process for five or more years is that their profits sky-rocket, they have a surprisingly minimal learning curve, and initial resistance is quickly overcome with the training we provide as part of the process. We've crafted this

solution specifically for this industry, with the understanding that the concept is pretty new. With your approval, may we complete this demo? It will take less than fifteen minutes ...

CUSTOMER: I just don't need all those bells and whistles.
YOU: Yes. You're right. There are a lot of bells and whistles! I never thought I'd use half of them either and I certainly didn't want to pay for them. When my hard drive crashed last year, and the data had been automatically backed up, those bells never sounded so sweet! Would you have five minutes anytime this week or next to see how they can provide peace of mind for just pennies a day?

PROSPECT: You're wrong. This won't work for us. It doesn't make any sense and your pricing is way out of the ballpark, when you include your shipping charges. We like our current supplier. I really see no reason to continue this conversation.
YOU: I respect what you're saying. We expect shipping costs to reduce significantly when our new plant opens in Nashville. Would it be fair if I contact you again in a year, after our distribution process is updated?

Learn to listen for agreement, show respect, and build your case around the customers' needs. Sincerely listen to what they have to say and watch your success and your sales blossom.

2

Using Tools of Persuasion

We may convince others by our arguments; but we can only persuade them by their own.
—Joseph Joubert

Whether you're old enough to remember the original TV program *Dragnet*, or you're young enough to catch the late-night reruns, you've probably heard Jack Webb, a.k.a Investigator Joe Friday, say, "Just the facts, ma'am. Just the facts."

A career in sales would be so easy if you only had to communicate the facts. If spewing data would beat the competition, if memorizing and reciting facts would boost revenue, if presenting features would build relationships, the world would be filled with successful salespeople. Of course, if selling were that easy, high-achieving salespeople wouldn't earn six-figure incomes, trips to the Amalfi Coast, or awards at recognition dinners.

In today's marketplace, it's so much more complicated than "just the facts." Selling means persuading people that, even though they may be perfectly happy the way they are now and with the processes currently in place, they'll be happier, more successful, richer, more beautiful, and have more time because of what you're offering them. No wonder we win trips to exotic locations!

It comes as no surprise that buyers can find the facts and make their decision to buy—or not—without you. These days, we can find anything we need to know just by Googling for information. It's having the skill to persuade, influence, and convince your buyer to accept your point of view that creates sales success. It doesn't matter whether your sales cycle is long or short, complex or simple. With the best words to convey confidence and help customers overcome their objections, you will be more successful at selling.

This chapter provides customer-centric communication tools and tips to help you increase your influence and control the sales conversation. I'll challenge some common misconceptions to help you use your time with your customer productively and profitably, instead of playing games. You'll see examples you can use (in your own words, of course) to make it easy and comfortable for your buyer to say yes. We'll explore new ways to convey power and professionalism so that, given multiple choices, your customer chooses to buy what *you* offer. The point is to keep the conversation going so that you can more deeply understand your customer's needs. When you accomplish that, whether your sales conversation takes place over the phone, face to face, or in email, you enhance persuasiveness and trust and enjoy greater success.

TALK ABOUT THE "ELEPHANT
IN THE ROOM"

In an age of universal deceit,
telling the truth is a revolutionary act.
—George Orwell

Selina Lo, CEO of Ruckus Wireless, sells routers and other wireless products. She knows that her product has some less than ideal features. Instead of hiding behind the truth and pretending that glitches don't exist, she opens her sales presentations talking about "the elephant in the room." According to *Inc.* magazine's February 2007 issue, she starts the conversation by saying, "We make the worst case suck less." She controls the sales conversation and persuades her buyers by addressing the reality—the elephant in the room.

When the elephant sits in the middle of the room—that is, an obvious problem that no one has the courage to acknowledge—everyone loses. Persuasive salespeople are the first to bring up the truth. They don't pretend reality doesn't exist—even when the truth (high prices, long delivery cycles, complicated learning curve, lack of conclusive results, etc.) can hurt their case. Instead, by talking about the truth, a truth that everyone knows anyway, they become a more credible source of information, more trusted by their clients.

Have you ever looked over a menu and just couldn't decide on an entrée? When that happens, have you asked the server for his opinion? If the server recommends the highest-priced item on the menu, you distrust him. You can't help but wonder if he's trying to up the meal costs so he gets a better tip. If, however, he says, "You know, the grouper is pretty expensive—the most expensive thing on the menu—but it's the best I've ever tasted. About a week ago, I served some folks from the Bahamas, and they said it was even better than they get there! The chef's preparation is amazing. If you want to spend that much, it's really worth it. Fish and chips [*a lower-priced item*] is also a great choice," he builds trust by addressing the "elephant in the room"—in this case, the high price. The most amazing thing is that now that he is seen as a trusted sales advisor, he can upsell his customers on salads, drinks, and desserts. He enhances his ability to persuade and influence.

The alternative to talking about an unfavorable truth, naturally, is to ignore it. Doing that decreases influence for two reasons:

1. If no one brings up an obvious problem, the sales conversation may have been easy for you, but a primary objection (the high price, for instance) wasn't addressed. The result? No influence and no sale.
2. If the prospect brings up the issue, she controls the conversation. She brings it up the way she wants, when she wants. You could be shaking hands with the vice president (who may have been the only person in the room unaware of your extremely high prices because he was out of the country when the news release broke) when the procurement officer walks over and quietly says to you, "I was very surprised you didn't mention the comparison published in the *Journal* last week. I was waiting for you to address it." Even if you discuss it right there and then, you've lost opportunity and credibility.

Here are three key steps to keep in mind:

Step 1. Purposefully plan to discuss an existing problem that might keep the customer from doing business with you.

Step 2. Counteract any negative perceptions he may have by quickly and clearly describing your more positive view of the situation. Make the "elephant" unimportant.

Step 3. Limit your comments to only what the buyer needs to know.

Direct, Clear, and Concise

When you talk about the elephant, you can address it most persuasively by remembering: DCC—direct, clear, and concise. Tell your customers what they need to know, eliminating details that aren't pertinent to them and the situation. Keep your words plain and your explanation simple. Avoid making the elephant not only loom larger, but start smelling, too, with "war" stories or information overload.

Example:

YOU: As you already know, on price point, we can't compete. If we're talking value and safety, we offer an unbeatable package.

In some instances, that will be enough. You bring up the uncomfortable truth and then dispel it with a value statement. Depending on your type of sale, however, you may need to go into greater depth. Regardless of how complex the issue, say it clearly and simply.

Example:

Let's say your call center was recently outsourced to another country and you have no idea if Sara, your contact, has heard the news. If you ignore the truth and carry on as if the center is still located in St. Paul, you know the sales conversation will be much less stressful for you. Of course, this also wouldn't be truthful.

You decide to take the high road to talk about the elephant, even though it would be much more pleasant to avoid the matter. You know this is a big issue to her. After initial pleasantries, you say in a direct, clear, and concise manner:

> **YOU: Sara, I don't know if you've heard that we've outsourced the call center. Some of our customers were pretty unhappy when they heard the news though almost everyone has come around now that they have a live person to speak to instead of being sent to voice mail hell. There is still some frustration with the language differences, and we're working on that. If it had been possible to offer the same level of service, and continue to offer our great pricing, we would have preferred to keep the jobs here.**

Sara is shocked by this news and angrily says: "That stinks, that really stinks."

What can you say? You can respond so that you keep the sales conversation moving forward. As we discussed in the previous chapter, authentically accept her words. Affirm her. Be clear and concise. Don't confuse her with extraneous information; keep the dialogue relevant by telling her only and exactly what she needs to know to understand the situation. Respond to her comment in a way that

helps her feel safe enough to continue telling you her opinion. You want to know what her questions, objections, and
feelings are about the "elephant."

> **YOU: You're right, it isn't the ideal—**
> **SARA (*cuts you off*): You're darn right, it isn't. This stinks**
> **big time.**

Good news! Your ability to listen for points of
agreement—see Chapter 1—disarmed her. You succeeded
in helping her feel comfortable enough to keep talking!
She didn't stonewall you and pull her account from your
hands.

> **YOU: Yes. Some other clients felt the same way at first.**
> **Most are pretty happy now because they're so pleased**
> **with how quickly they get thorough answers.**
> **SARA (*sarcastically*): Well, I'm not "most customers." I'm**
> **not sure I'll ever come around. You know how important**
> **it is to both me and this company to keep things on this**
> **shore.**

Step back to defuse Sara's anger. Persuade her to continue
talking to you by first accepting her viewpoint, and next, answering her unspoken question: "Do you know how important this is to both me and this company?" Keep her talking
and you move forward. Anger her with ill-spoken words,
and she refuses to do business with you.

> **YOU (*respectfully*): Yes, your company is well known for**
> **its stand on outsourcing and that is why I wanted to per-**
> **sonally tell you about the center, and the services we can**

now provide. **The fact that fully researched and documented answers are guaranteed within twelve hours—and they're averaging an eight-hour response time—and that your people can get back to their customers with the information they need the very next day, is a huge positive.**

Sara may or may not, in the end, come around. Your only chance to persuade her, to influence her to see your viewpoint, comes from addressing the elephant directly, clearly, and concisely.

Stack the deck in your favor by being the first to speak the truth.

Selling is one of the most honorable jobs on the planet, when it's done honorably. By addressing the elephant in the room, you create an environment of trust and openness. I'm not suggesting your customers will be thrilled to hear about that elephant, but when you take the initiative to discuss it, they'll respect you. That respect translates into an opportunity to persuade them to see your point of view.

Use Humor to Address the Elephant

Ronald Reagan was seventy-three and running for reelection against the younger Walter Mondale. He was the oldest president to serve the first time he ran, and during the first presidential debate, it seemed his age was showing. He made a few mistakes and admitted to being "confused." In the next debate, however, he ended all concern that he was too old for the office when he joked, "I want you to know that also I will not make age an issue of this campaign. I am not going to exploit, for political purposes, my opponent's youth and inexperience." Even Mondale had to smile at the humorous and clever way that Reagan addressed the elephant.

Humor is a tool of persuasion. Used appropriately, it changes attitudes, improves credibility, and distracts from a negative issue. When we laugh together, we relax, open up, and connect.

A misconception many salespeople have, however, is that humor is also universal. Not so fast, milk breath! (See what I mean? Someone, somewhere found that funny!) What plays in Vegas isn't going to work in Salt Lake City. And what New Yorkers might find hysterical, Southerners might find less than charming.

How to Say It to ensure the successful use of persuasive humor:

- Tell stories. Stories are persuasive because they're universal. Record funny things that happen to you. It's been said that truth is stranger than fiction. It's funnier, too. Write down funny situations you encounter. Think about how they can help you prove your point or diffuse a negative situation. Leave out the parts of the story that aren't that funny or don't help drive your point. Practice your story until you can make your friends and family laugh with you (not at you).

- Plan for humor. Spontaneous humor usually isn't. It's been created, crafted, and rehearsed so frequently that it sounds natural and spontaneous.

- Avoid jokes. If the joke is any good, they've heard it. If it isn't, you're likely to offend someone. Additionally (if you decide to ignore this tip), never tell a joke as if it were a true occurrence. If your prospect heard the joke before, you lose all credibility. Instead of being persuasive, you lose face.

- Laugh at your own expense. Self-deprecating humor is a particularly effective way to dispel the elephant in the room. When your customers can laugh along with you, you create a basis for memorable relationships.
- Being clever is sometimes easier than being funny. Playfully point out your competition's weakness. For example, my local Dunkin Donuts coffee shop is located three doors away from a Starbucks. A huge banner outside Dunkin Donuts persuades customers to choose them: "Only the coffee needs to be rich." They don't mention the competition directly, yet everyone knows the elephant they're talking about.

TELL THEM WHAT YOU CAN DO—
NOT WHAT YOU CAN'T

A pleasant sales conversation makes selling easier and buying more fun. When we hear encouraging, positive words, we not only feel more comfortable, we become more receptive to the message. Current research indicates that the human brain literally shows different response patterns to messages presented in negative or positive frameworks.

Because your choice of words increases the probability of making the sale, avoiding negative words, or those with negative overtones and connotations, is essential. Sometimes, though, it's difficult to recognize when we're not being positive. Studies, involving both verbal communications and email, highlight that most of us are guilty of significantly overestimating our ability to convey our intent to another. So here's some help!

To connect with your buyer, as briefly mentioned in the previous chapter, avoid these two words in any sales conversation: "no" and "but."

Saying yes when you mean no is counterproductive. It's not smart business to agree to what you can't do. You can, however, eliminate *saying* the word "no," by instead telling the customer what *is* possible.

When you begin a response with "no," you place the sales dialogue in jeopardy because the buyer may not be able to see past your refusal. Instead of listening to what you're saying, he's likely to either close down entirely, or concentrate on his rebuttal to your negative response. Either way, he isn't listening or learning anything new from you. The sales dialogue stops. The challenge is that most of us *automatically*—without thinking—say "no" when we're asked a yes-no question and our answer is no. Yet we usually follow that negative word with something positive:

Is it raining out? *No*, it's sunny today.
Will this plan cover the entire family? *No*, only your spouse and any children under the age of eighteen.

Eliminate saying no and you change your world for two reasons. You:

- Enable your customer to save face, increasing your ability to persuade him.
- Present yourself as a more positive, likable business professional.

Nixing the word "no" from your vocabulary is easier said than done. Try this:

1. Become aware of how often you currently respond with the word "no."
2. Be *willing* to eliminate "no" from your vocabulary (unless you must stop your two-year-old from running into the street).
3. Much like you counteract negativity when overcoming the elephant in the room by discussing a more positive view of the situation, you can refrain from saying "no" by talking about what is possible, not what isn't.

Because changing such an ingrained habit like saying "no" can be so challenging, it's sometimes easier to use a substitute word. A simple way to avoid saying "no" is to replace it with the word "actually." The substitute word, "actually," becomes a place holder: a way to avoid falling into the trap of starting a response negatively. By making this replacement, you also shift the focus of the statement. You enable your buyer to listen more readily to your explanation, rather than making her want to defend her dignity or point of view.

CLIENT: Will these work as well in extreme temperatures?
YOU: *Actually*, the function is slightly diminished in temperatures above 105 degrees Fahrenheit and below 5 degrees Fahrenheit. We can compensate for that by adding the converter we talked about.
CLIENT: But you aren't going to just "throw in" the converter, are you?

YOU: *Actually*, with a twelve-month finance plan, we can offer it to you for pennies on the dollar. It would add roughly $X a day for full functionality.

Sometimes using the word "if" is helpful in moving the conversation forward. This is particularly useful when you'd really like to say "yes" (and if there were any way you could, you would), but can't. An "if-I" construction communicates this true desire and is both persuasive and powerful.

Example:

Your prospect asks for additional concessions, and it's not possible for you to grant them the way your offer is currently structured. If he doesn't move from the existing deal on the table, you have no wiggle room. This example shows three equally persuasive responses:

PROSPECT: I'm going to need additional concessions to take to my client. Can you do that?

YOU: *Yes*. By extending the commitment to a month or more, I can offer you those additional concessions.

OR: *Actually*, I can grant additional concessions with a month or more commitment.

OR: *If I* could provide them for you, I'd be happy to do that. What I can do for you is . . .

The purpose of these communication strategies and word tracks is to keep the dialogue going. You're not trying to trick, or pressure, a customer into anything.

BUYER: I can get what you're offering on the Internet without going through your extensive approval process. Can't you expedite this?

YOU: Actually, the up-front approval process enables you to purchase up to $100,000 without any additional credit check.

BUYER: I don't need that much credit. I just want to be able to make my purchases without having to deal with all this paperwork. You came to see me because you said you had such a great deal. Can't you do anything for me?

YOU: If I could, I'd be happy to. We've found that this up-front process, in the long run, saves you time and money because . . .

BUYER: I have no budget for this. Can you do it for me without charging me this time?

YOU: Actually, I limit my free speaking engagements to ten nonprofit organizations each year.

BUYER: Come on, it's only forty-five minutes.

YOU: Yes, and if I could figure out a way to do that for you, I'd be honored to do it. My standard fee is . . .

In this next example, notice how, using a combination of the communication skills we've discussed so far, you're able to manage the conversation and move away from a potentially explosive situation.

CUSTOMER: Would you be willing to sponsor a golf hole for our charity event?

YOU: *Actually*, what I can do is volunteer that day and help out.

CUSTOMER: No, that isn't what I asked you. I asked if your company would ante up and sponsor a hole to help us out.

YOU: *If* I could, I definitely would.

CUSTOMER: Then why can't you? We bring you a lot of business.

YOU: *You're right*, you do—and we do appreciate it! We're major donors to Give Kids the World and also sponsor the MS walk, and other events. As a corporate team, we get together every two years to decide where to put our sponsorship dollars and offer community service. I'd really like to help out, so if you need another body that day, you can count on me. (You might add: And I'd be happy to put your name into our hat the next time we meet about this.)

"If-I" is a positive construction. "If-you" isn't. Use "when-you" instead of "if-you" to present your message in a more positive and persuasive manner.

INSTEAD OF: *If* you make the deposit, I'll send the materials.
BETTER: *When* you make the deposit, I'll send the materials.

INSTEAD OF: *If* you call, I'll complete the reservation.
BETTER: *When* you call, I'll complete the reservation.

INSTEAD OF: *If* you can get the approvals, I'll provide the data.
BETTER: *When* you get the approvals, I'll provide the data.

The word "but" also diminishes the ability to be persuasive when it devalues the first part of the sentence. Replace "but" with "and" and both parts of the sentence will have equal positive value. This creates a more persuasive statement and a more pleasant sales conversation.

Example:

Your customer asks you to add four hundred more palettes to his order. Normally, you'd be thrilled but you pushed your shipping department to rush the original order and they just can't get the entire order to him by his deadline. The additional palettes will need to ship at a later date. Notice how, in the following response, the word "but" deflates the fact that you do have a solution and can do what he wants:

YOU: We can do that, *but* **those four hundred palettes will arrive as a separate shipment three to five days later.**

The word "and" is more positive and more persuasive:

YOU: Yes, we can add those four hundred palettes, *and* **we'll ship those separately, three to five days later.**

ELIMINATE COMMON SELLING MISTAKES

There are few things more persuasive than offering respect. Respect helps you grow your business, build relationships, and boost sales. Yet along the way, many salespeople have picked up habits that aren't as respectful, strong, or influential as they could be. Maybe you were taught manipulative strategies by old-school sales trainers (strategies that may have worked successfully in a shortsighted "win the business whatever it takes" mentality), or are so busy trying to make a living that you haven't had time to stop to consider if your sales "arsenal" might contain a few bombs that need diffusing. Many sales folks, even today, are quickly sent out on their own after observing a colleague make a sales presentation, or doing a "ride-along" for a day or two. You repeat the same "skills" your colleague learned three months or thirty years earlier.

One of the most common mistakes salespeople make is to disregard respect as a tool of persuasion. Please don't misunderstand. I am not advocating that you fake it to gain a sales edge. My recommendation is that you find a way to convey the respect you truly feel for your client, every time you communicate. Do this and you'll separate yourself from your competitive set. In any sales conversation, when mutual trust and respect are present, when both the buyer and the seller are actively involved in truthful conversation, relationships and sales abound. These tips will help you create that type of conversation so that you won't have to push to be persuasive.

We've looked at various ways of speaking respectfully and persuasively. By eliminating "salesy" types of communication behaviors and helping your customer feel more comfortable by listening for agreement, being truthful and clear about any perceived negative situation, and using words that don't demean their viewpoint, you can create a respectful, high-trust relationship. Now, we'll look at common selling mistakes to avoid because they detract from your natural persuasion abilities.

Don't Answer a Question with a Question

Some sales techniques are manipulative and disrespectful. One such "cheesy" behavior is answering a buyer's question with a question of your own. When your customer asks a question, he deserves the best answer you can give him. That doesn't mean you must give him an answer you don't yet have. If he wants to know costs, and you need more information from him before you can accurately respond, you can't provide the answer to his question. You can, however, give him an answer that demonstrates that you heard what he said and that you value his need to have the answer. Often what happens is that salespeople want to keep the conversation flowing on *their* schedule; they want to build value before offering price. Being respectful means providing answers when the customer wants them—not when you're ready to give them.

How to Say It:
1. Respond as best you can to the question.
2. Next, ask your fact-finding question.
3. If she comes back to the question, again answer honestly and respectfully. Tell what you do know about the answer before gathering more information from her.
4. Make it clear to your customer that you have her best interests in mind. To do this, of course, you must really care about her concerns, needs and success, and not just about your own interests. Ask yourself, How can I show my buyers that I care about what they want?

Example:
PROSPECT: Hmmm ... Can I ask you what the costs are?
YOU: Yes, of course. The costs are dependent on the number of books ordered, and the frequency with which you'll be ordering. How many books do you estimate needing?

PROSPECT: Truthfully, before I waste your time hearing more, I need to know costs. We're comfortable with our current supplier and the delivery process, and I'm not willing to increase the budget in this area at this time.

YOU: Ballpark, again depending on the number of books ordered and the frequency with which you'll be ordering, the costs can range from $XXX to $XXXX.

Avoid the Presumptive Close

Another less than honorable sales technique is known as "the presumptive close." Salespeople who use this close, like the snake oil salesmen who came before them, attempt to fool their customers into saying yes. In wrapping up the sales conversation, the salesperson presumes (or assumes) that the prospect has already decided to buy and talks to her as if the purchase is complete. This behavior makes it difficult for the buyer to say no. The sad fact is that it can work for the short-term one-transaction sale. Salespeople who know that their presentation isn't persuasive (because the product isn't good or the prospect has no need for it) use it to *push* the buyer into saying yes. The salesperson never expects to do business with or see the customer again (picture the sheriff and his posse running 'em out of town!), so (manipulative) persuasion—not respectful behavior—is paramount.

These three examples should be enough to demonstrate how not to say it. Notice how they usually include some sort of flattery.

- I wish I could be with you to see the look on your wife's face when you walk in with these earrings for her. (*Salesperson has presumed you're purchasing them.*)

- *When the prospect is looking at the yellow flowerpots being offered:* So I see you looking at these yellow ones. They're beauties! (*Putting them into a bag*) What great taste you have! Would you like three or four of these?
- We can get going on this before your next meeting. *This usually comes after the salesperson has asked a series of yes-no questions so the prospect has been prepared for the kill, such as:*

  - "Do you agree?"
  - "Does this make sense to you?"
  - "Is that also true here?"
  - "I'm sure you've also experienced that?" (*Said as a question, waiting for a yes.*)

Closing the sale should be a natural outgrowth of your sales conversation. An extremely simplified explanation of the sales process looks like this:

- You locate a prospect with a need for a product like yours.
- You determine/confirm that your product satisfies her needs.
- You offer the product in an honest and respectful manner.
- She has questions, objections, or conflicting opinions.
- You help her to see that her objections are unwarranted because of the solutions you offer.
- You suggest the next logical step, which could be a purchase, conference call, meeting with additional team members, proposal submittal, etc.

- She buys or moves to the next step.
- You follow up.

If it feels cheesy saying it, it is. Don't say it.

Clarify Without Mimicking

Mimicking is another sales strategy that gives selling and
salespeople a bad name. The customer says something, and
the salesperson repeats it, verbatim, typically beginning
with something like, "So, if I understand you correctly . . ."

The clarification process *is* important because it's very
possible that you heard a different message than what was
said. Mimicking, however, is not the best way to accomplish this. Communicate respect, and enhance your influence at the same time, by clarifying what the client says
to you without repeating his words. Instead of parroting
back exactly what you just heard, expand the sales conversation by integrating new information into your clarification step.

Example:

**CLIENT: Okay, this sounds good. We'll give these products
a test run. Send me twelve pieces and I'll see what the
team thinks.**

**YOU: Great! So then after your team works with the twelve
pieces that I send you, what would you like the next step to
be? May I host your debrief meeting so I can hear their
feedback?**

**BUYER: I'm not sure this will work for us because we're
pretty locked in with our methodology.**

YOU: Okay. The methodology you're using has been standard operating procedure. Are you getting all the results you'd like?

Do not say:

So what I heard you say is . . .
So, if I understand you clearly, A, B, and C are important
    to you. Is that correct?
What I'm hearing you want is A, B, C . . .

NOBODY WINS WITH WIN-WIN

In an ideal world, every sales conversation would end with each party receiving exactly what he wants, and everyone would enjoy a win-win sale. Realistically, however, your customers aren't that interested in a win-win. They're interested in winning.

A hotel company I work with had taught their sales leaders to say to their corporate prospects, "We'd like to make this a win-win for both of us." Their intention was admirable: Let's *both* win. In reality, win-win is as elusive as a happy compromise; it doesn't exist. One party—or both—*gives up* something originally desired to come to an agreeable solution. The underlying message, in a sales presentation based on win-win, is that the customer will need to forfeit some of his needs to reach a common ground. You risk alienating him.

Keep the focus of your conversation on how he will win. Direct all your efforts to helping him enjoy victory in the (unspoken) negotiation. It's not that you both may not win; you may. But as the universe will have it, the more you can help the *customer* win, the more you will, too.

Instead of win-win, focus on the customer's success:

- Discuss the solution in terms of how he benefits only.
- Avoid any discussion of a win-win solution.

Notice how the powerful choices in these examples focus exclusively on the buyer.

POOR CHOICES	POWERFUL CHOICES
We'd like to make this a win-win.	We'd like to help you create the most successful . . .
We're pleased to partner with you . . .	We're pleased to provide this service to you . . .
This is a mutually beneficial solution.	This solution saves you time, money . . .

Before using a sales "technique," consider if it's respectful as well as persuasive.

ALIGN YOUR BODY LANGUAGE WITH YOUR WORDS

Though nonverbal, we all know that sometimes body language communicates volumes. It either reinforces our words and enhances our ability to be persuasive or works against our message. From the way we sit at the sales meeting, to a quick roll of the eyes, or an audible sigh, we telegraph whether we believe what we, or our customers, are saying.

When words and actions offer contradictory meaning, we tend to believe the actions (hence the adage "Actions speak louder than words"). Knowing this, it's crucial to pay attention to your own body language so that it's as persuasive as your words.

Here's how to say it to let your customer know you respect what she's saying:

1. Nod your head in an encouraging "yes" manner. Imagine that you're saying "yes, please go on," with your head.
2. Eliminate any negative head nod.
3. Smile appropriately. Nothing is as respectful and persuasive as an authentic smile.
4. Keep your body still. Avoid tapping your foot, or crossing or swinging your leg. No matter how long it's taking a buyer to make her point, show respect. Maintain self-control and eliminate pen clicking, twirling your ring, and running your fingers through your hair. Any repetitive body movement can look like you're perplexed, bored, or frustrated.
5. Lean in to show that you're listening and that her words are important to you. Of course, you shouldn't be on top of her! Keeping your body forward in your chair in an alert position is far more engaging than sitting back, arms splayed over the back of your chair.

Your body language must indicate that you're fully engaged and focused on the customer. In that way, you more easily persuade and encourage her to stay engaged. Anything less than your full attention is insulting.

Persuading is hard work, and creating an environment of trust is crucial to sales success. The tools we've discussed in this chapter enable your sales conversation to continue. You'll enhance your ability to influence and persuade your buyers when your words and behaviors demonstrate that you care about them and their goals. Help them to trust your selling motives by selling respectfully and staying focused on their success.

3

Become Your Customer to Sell It

*If you just learn a single trick, Scout, you'll get along
a lot better with all kinds of folks. You never really
understand a person until you consider things from
his point of view . . . Until you climb inside of his
skin and walk around in it.*
—Harper Lee, *To Kill a Mockingbird*

Understanding the true needs and wants of your prospects is arguably the most important part of the sales process. When their desires, goals, and objectives are the focus of the sale, instead of *your* product, service, or idea, you're at your persuasive best. When you talk about what matters to *them* and what will help *them* create greater success, keeping the sales conversation going is easy. Instead of being in the position of trying to convince them to do something they may not be interested in doing, you're helping them see that you're the best option to help them get what they want.

Tom Monaghan, founder of Domino's Pizza and a devout Roman Catholic, understood this fact. He knew that treating people as *he* would like to be treated might not yield the best sales results. He built his company on his policy of "Golden Rule Management," which he defined as, "Do unto others as *they* would like to be done unto." What Monaghan discovered was that what he might be most interested in when deciding to buy a pizza—the way it tastes, the quality and consistency of product—was not necessarily what mattered most to his buyers. To many pizza buyers, a hot pizza delivered quickly to their door was more important than the pizza's taste. Monaghan guaranteed that it would arrive within thirty minutes after being ordered. If Domino's Pizza had sold its product based on what mattered most to the company's founder, chances are the company may not have achieved the success it enjoyed.

Customer-centric communication, as we've been discussing, revolves around the customer in every way. Whether it's an email message, a face-to-face meeting, a formal presentation, or a sales culture like Domino's, those who sell more, more easily, keep the sales conversation focused on the buyer's need.

Additionally, the *way* you say *what* you say must align with the manner in which your buyers best receive information. More than a question of whether you should send an email or place a phone call, you need to sell to your customer in the way she would like to be sold to. When you understand how she accepts and processes information, as well as how she's most comfortable staying involved in the sales conversation, you can best deliver your message. To get the sales result you desire, step into your customer's mind-set.

PAY ATTENTION TO YOUR PROSPECT

Customers participating in a customer-centric dialogue think, "Wow, this salesperson gets what I want." If I'm planning a trip to Australia, for example, and I call a travel agent for info, he won't try to sell me specially priced flights to Spain. In the same way, salespeople selling any product, service, or idea must craft their conversations to fit the individual client's specific objectives and sell what that customer needs, not what they have for sale.

Salespeople often believe it's in the customer's best interest to mention their most exciting product features. Because, and I hear this all the time in my sales training workshops, "Maybe they don't know about the new product," or "Maybe it will be a selling point," or "If I don't tell them about it, maybe I'll lose the sale." This seems to make sense until you realize that providing information without finding out if there is a need (or if the prospect even cares) is no different than a doctor prescribing allergy medicine because his drug rep told him it was a fabulous new drug! Even if the patient needed allergy medicine, and simply forgot to mention it because he was there for a broken toe, the doctor would have to ask questions to find out his need. When information is provided just because, it isn't in the customer's best interest at all; it's only in the salesperson's best interest.

Keep these ideas in mind to stay focused on your customer's motives for buying:

1. Listen. Customers tell you exactly how and what they'd like to buy from you. Don't discount what they have to say!

2. Keep in mind that no matter how fabulous your new product is, it is meaningless to them unless they have a need for that new product at this time.

3. Without being patronizing, ask them for their approval to ask questions to uncover their needs. Pose specific questions about the outcome they envision. You might want to provide a sentence of background to explain why you're probing for more information, such as:

I'm not certain that I'm the best speaker for your meeting! May I ask you a few questions about your group and what you'd like them to do differently or better after they've listened to the keynote speech?

You say you'd like your garden to be beautiful. I can do that! To help me design the perfect landscape for you, would you describe "beautiful"? For instance, when you look out your window, would it be more beautiful to you to see shade trees or colorful bushes?

I believe I understand what you're looking for. With your approval, may I confirm what I've learned from my preliminary research?

Example:

You are the sales manager for the ABC Hotel. The hotel just completed a $6 million renovation. Most of the money went to building an incredible new spa and tennis complex. You're delighted when the association executive of Cute Pups calls to see if you have twelve rooms and a boardroom available December 18–19.

YOU: Yes! We have rooms and suites available for those nights, and our beautiful boardroom is also available. May I ask what type of meeting you're planning?

CUSTOMER: It's a strategic planning meeting for our entire board.
YOU: Will they be in the meeting all day or will they have time to visit our new spa and tennis complex?
CUSTOMER: They'll be in meetings from 7 a.m. until 7 p.m. All work and no pleasure at this meeting.

As you can see, there would be no need to tell him about the new spa even though it is the most wonderful part of the hotel experience. It doesn't matter to your customer.

To keep the sales conversation flowing, everything you say must focus on the customer, his needs, and his desired outcomes.

SELL TO CUSTOMERS THE WAY THEY WANT TO BUY

It's only natural to believe that our work habits and routines are the best way to accomplish results. (Okay . . . some of us are aware that not all of our habits may always be worth modeling!) If we love email, for instance, we tend to think our customers do, too. If we prefer talking on the phone, we assume they like it just as much. If it's served us well to meet customers in person, we figure they'll understand how important that is, too.

Depending on our preferred communication style (which we'll discuss below), our age, gender, culture, and even the sales training we've been through, we've developed methods with which we're comfortable both buying and selling. Undoubtedly, some of us are more flexible than others, yet we still have our preferences. Your customers do, too.

An insurance salesman told me that a large software company's employees are the bulk of his customer base. "It drives me crazy," he said, "because all they want to do is communicate by email. I know I could sell more and do a better job for them if they'd just talk to me."

The insurance agent, if he really believes that he could serve his customers better, needs to persuade his customers on the value *they'll* get from meeting with him face-to-face.

And making that case for the meeting value will be extraordinarily difficult because the customer doesn't prefer to meet! The agent's customers, mainly younger and more computer savvy than him, may simply prefer to change agents if he stresses how much more successfully *he* can serve them if they meet. His selling methods don't mesh with their buying methods. In the end, he will keep the sales conversation going only by taking good care of them entirely the way they prefer.

A surefire way to lose customers is to ignore the signs that point to their preferred method of communication. Enhance your flexibility to carry on the sales conversation in the way that is convenient for your customer, no matter how far is strays from your ideal way of communicating. Be prepared with a strong knowledge of your product's selling points and be ready to talk about them in any communication medium rather than relying on a specific way of delivering the information.

Example:

Imagine that you're at dinner with a prospect named Pamela. She has shown interest in investing in your project based on the recommendation of two current investors, both friends of hers. *You* are most comfortable first getting to know each other over dinner and then, after coffee and dessert, bringing up the investment opportunity. Yet seconds after you sit down, Pamela says to you, "Phil, I want to know, bottom line, how this will impact the environment. That is, first and foremost, what's important to me. After that, tell me about the project design and what it will cost me to invest. Finally, tell me how the profit structure will look."

You aren't ready to talk business at this point but Pamela is, so you wisely put away the agenda you had in mind and begin your sales conversation. Even though you know the most compelling aspect of the project is its design, and you had planned to lead off with that (after dinner), you know you must begin with the project's impact on the environment. She clearly told you that was the most important thing to her. You hesitate because you know that it (the environmental issue) is your weakest selling point and you would prefer not to begin with it. Honoring what matters to her, however, you open your conversation with her main concern. As it turns out, you already know how to do this (see Chapter 2, "Talk About the 'Elephant in the Room'"). You quickly move to your solution to overcome her objection to the elephant and proceed to answer her questions, in the order she wants to hear them.

Your customers will often tell you exactly how you can persuade them to buy from you. They tell you what their needs are, what matters most to them, and what doesn't impact the sale. They also tell you *how* they're most comfortable communicating. Sell to them in a customer-centric, not ego-centric, manner so they can process the information you present in the way that works best for them.

ADAPT YOUR COMMUNICATION STYLE TO THEIRS

We see the world through a filter of experiences and beliefs. To connect with customers, then, it's important to understand how they filter your messages. The more you understand how they communicate and process information, the more likely you are to be persuasive and influential.

The first step is to determine your own communication style:

Are you an open or closed communicator?
Are you direct or indirect?

An open communicator readily and expressively shares thoughts and feelings. He's outgoing, makes eye contact easily, and holds back neither his thoughts nor his feelings. A closed communicator is more reserved and keeps her distance both emotionally and physically. Until she gets to know you well, direct eye contact can be difficult for her.

Consider how annoying it could be to a highly closed communicator to be approached by a highly open salesperson. The salesperson is bright and cheery and talkative. Maybe she opens her sales conversation by talking about something personal that happened to her that morning. To her, she is revealing a bit of herself to bond with this prospect. The closed communicator may not only be embarrassed by the story, but may also be appalled by the salesperson's approach. He may think, "We just met. Why are you telling me this? What does this have to do with my business or yours?"

What about the reverse? Though it's true that the majority of salespeople tend to lean more toward the open side of the communication spectrum, highly closed communicators also must sell. If a reserved salesperson walks in and talks about her project dispassionately, the open buyer might think, "Well, if she doesn't even believe in this, I'm sure not going to buy in. She can't work up enough enthusiasm to smile? And didn't she notice the great tie I'm wearing?"

A good way to distinguish these styles is to think "Open—Emotional" and "Closed—Quiet."

OPEN	CLOSED
Relationship-driven	Facts, please
Outgoing	Reserved
Animated	Still
Competitive	Cooperative

The other factor impacting communication style centers on directness or indirectness. Direct people communicate as the name implies: directly. They see and speak in terms of black-and-white solutions allowing for few gray possibilities, are competitive, and tend to be controlling. In sales meetings, expect them to speak more loudly than others (often intimidating to indirect buyers), and to argue for their point. Direct communicators are also known as "high-involvement" communicators because they are so involved in the communication that they respond to your points even while you make them. They talk over you and expect you to persevere and overcome their objections by confidently talking over them in return, if you truly believe in your message.

Indirect communicators are not confrontational. Called "high-considerateness" speakers, they allow you to speak and they wait their turn to avoid stepping over your words or on your toes. Because considerateness is what guides them, they are likely to say nothing if they disagree with you to avoid conflict. They aren't interested in being competitive (they prefer to get their way in a nonconfrontational manner), and like the status quo to taking risks.

Extremely indirect and extremely direct people communicate their messages entirely differently. These behaviors are easy to differentiate.

DIRECT	INDIRECT
Blunt	Sensitively chosen words
Confrontational	Accepting
Pushy	Polite
Fast paced	Slow paced
Loud	Quiet

As you can imagine, if your communication style is highly direct (a "pushy" New Yorker) and your buyer is highly indirect (a "slow" Southerner), adapting your communication style (whether you're the "pushy" or the "slow" one) to the *customer's* style is critical. When styles clash, sales are lost.

It's possible to be both direct and open, and direct and closed. Furthermore, you can be indirect and open or indirect and closed. Here are the four combinations and

How to Say It to reduce resistance to your communication style:

Expressives or Socializers (Direct and Open)

These people are both blunt and emotional. Because of this, it's vital to find a way to accept their ideas. (Use Chapters 1 and 2's tips to help move the conversation forward in times of conflict.) Don't you waste their time, but do listen to their stories, and let your sales conversation flow around them. Do not expect to stick to a rigid agenda. Ask for their advice, which they'll readily give, and encourage discussion. (Not much encouragement will be needed!) Your sales conversation should include testimonials from prestigious people and well-known companies to appeal to their desire for status. Because they tend to make decisions rapidly—very much dependent on whether they like you and trust you—reassure them of their wise buying decision with follow-up emails and phone calls.

Drivers or Directors (Direct and Closed)

Appealing to bottom-line results is the best way to sell to this blunt, fast-paced, and reserved style. Given the mix of attributes, this group is aggressive and singularly focused on results, with little concern about the feelings of the people responsible for giving them those results. It's important not to waste their time, especially talking about personal issues or providing fun vignettes! You'll persuade and impress this group by amping up the pace of your presentation, getting straight to the point, presenting ideas in a logical flow, eliminating emotional appeal, strictly honoring time commitments, and always seeing things from their viewpoint (tools discussed previously in Chapter 2).

Follow up with a bullet-point email highlighting the results they can expect to achieve from their buying decision.

Analyticals or Thinkers (Indirect and Closed)

Slower-paced and reserved, these people place extreme importance on thoroughness and accuracy. Their workspace is neat and structured, and their reports are, too. Consequently, your sales conversation must flow logically from one idea to the next. Come prepared with an agenda and tick off each point as it's discussed. Don't skip around points, and if you must, tell them you will circle back to complete the agenda—and remember to. These people require facts, figures, and specific details to be persuaded. They aren't interested in relationship building, and the fact that they might like you will have little bearing on their buying decision. Following up with this group is not critical, unless you said you would, because your conversation was so thorough that there is little left to discuss or confirm.

Amiables or Relators (Indirect and Open)

These people are the most pleasant to deal with because they are cooperative, relationship focused, and friendly. They want others to be happy and are more concerned about everyone getting along than on making perfect buying decisions. It's likely that as long as the rest of the committee thinks that your idea or product will help the department flourish, even if they disagree, they'll remain quiet and agreeable. Be pushy or aggressive with this type of communicator, though, and you can kiss the sale good-bye. They are so uncomfortable with that type of behavior that they'll remain silent, thank you, and avoid responding to your follow-up calls. Slow your pace, provide testimonials, ask them to invite other team members to the meeting, schedule meetings over meals or coffee, and always bring the sales conversation back to how your idea improves, enhances, and solidifies personal relationships. Follow up with them with a handwritten note that is focused on the pleasant meeting before launching into a recap of the ideas discussed.

By modifying the way you present your message, you increase your ability to extend your influence. Here's How to Say It to build connection with people unlike you:

1. Identify your communication pattern. Determine on a scale of 1–10 if you're an open or closed communicator. All of us lean more toward one style or the other. Avoid ranking yourself as a 5 because most likely it just isn't true. (Ask others to rank you on this scale if you really aren't certain of how you appear.)

2. Now, rate yourself 1–10 on your level of directness or indirectness. Again, be honest and avoid the middle of the road.

3. When you enter a sales conversation, be ready to assess your customers on both scales and try to become aware of how your communication styles differ.

4. Recognize how you might sound to them.

5. Mirror their communication patterns. If you're direct and open, for instance, and your customer is the opposite (indirect and closed), consciously lower your voice, pause between sentences, reduce animation, and avoid interrupting. If you're indirect and closed, try to speak more loudly, more quickly, and more forcefully.

Once you create a relationship bond, you can slowly return to your more comfortable style. By this point, your customer is willing to deal with your "idiosyncrasies" because she knows you have her best interests in mind.

Example:

Imagine you and your director of sales are at a networking event. You see your prospective client standing by herself by the door. Because both of you are expressives, you each wave a giant hello to her across the room. She sees you and tentatively smiles, waves back with a tiny little movement of her hand, and then looks away. You both walk over to her, but the music is very loud. You shout to be heard over the music and step in close to her to hear her response. Each time you step closer, she steps back and is now both literally and figuratively with her back against the wall.

Had you identified her as an indirect and closed communicator, you would have handled this communication differently. To have a productive sales conversation with her, it would be best to:

- Approach her singly (one of you will need to politely move away).
- Ask her if she'd like to step out of the ballroom into the foyer so you can talk quietly and not have to shout over the music.
- Stay out of her comfort zone of space.
- Speak slowly and calmly.
- Pause often to give her time to process your words and respond rather than frantically trying to fill in all gaps of silence.
- Avoid interrupting her or completing her sentences.
- Avoid providing personal information.
- Present information in a manner that allows her to voice her opinion without having to disagree with you.

- Reduce hand movements and other animated gestures.
- Avoid words that might sound argumentative.

Becoming customer-centric means eliminating a one-size-fits-all approach to selling. Every customer buys differently, has different needs, and comes to the sales conversation with different expectations. We do him an injustice when we offer a solution that isn't specific to his needs or present information in a way that isn't easy for him to grasp. Naturally, we do ourselves a disservice, too. Change that by mentally "climbing inside the other person's skin." Drive revenue and create customers who are "raving fans" by communicating in a way that makes it comfortable for them to buy. Accommodate their style by adjusting your own, and not only will you improve your odds of getting your message through, but you'll be likely to beat your quota, build meaningful relationships, and skyrocket your sales success.

PART II

Selling It on the Phone

One of the fastest ways to generate leads and create new business is through successful cold calling. But most salespeople hate cold calling and will do anything to avoid it. Yes, cold calling can be challenging and full of rejection. As much as you may have heard "don't take it personally," you do, because it just about always feels like you—not the company—are being personally rejected.

Common challenges such as starting with the right words, evaluating prospects to see if they're REAL, creating voice mail messages they'll want to return, and presenting your pitch without sounding like you're reading from a script are worth overcoming. When you can pick up the phone confidently, you'll dramatically increase your business opportunities and profits.

Part II helps you use the phone to your advantage by showing you how to qualify prospects, plan your cold call objective, generate leads, and make sales. You'll also learn how to use the phone to maintain relationships, respond to and create winning voice mail messages, and differentiate who you are and what you sell from your competition.

4

Cold Calling with Confidence

Ask. What's the worst that can happen?
All they can say is no.
—Philip Hershkowitz

Successful cold calling requires a great deal of preparation and the right attitude. Believing you can make the sale, however, is complicated by the fact that cold callers are so frequently told "no" that we often begin to sell to "no" without realizing it. Change the way you look at calling and you'll change the results you receive.

Once the right vision is in place, cold calling is a multi-step process you can master. The steps in the process are:

- Determine what result you want from the call.
- Prepare relevant questions to keep the prospect engaged.
- Plan your approach, pitch, and closing step.
- Find REAL prospects.
- Make the call.

We'll explore each of these steps.

EXPECT YES!

How often do you pick up the phone expecting the caller to say "no, not now, can't do"? Think about it, please, because here's the greatest challenge you need to overcome if you want to make successful sales calls: stop planning for a no. Here, instead, is what I want you to remember. Prospects are likely to say yes if:

- They need what you sell.
- You're prepared to sell it to them.
- You have an attitude of positive expectancy.

Believe What You're Saying and Selling

Certainly, a positive attitude won't make the sale without the other two components of the customer's need and your preparation. But without a positive attitude, it's highly doubtful you'll persuade anyone to do anything. The first of Warren Greshes's "Rock-Solid" rules, in his book *The Best Damn Sales Book Ever*, is, "Successful salespeople *see* themselves successful. They create visions." Without that vision, nothing happens.

It's not as though you have to shake your fist in the air screaming at the top of your lungs while walking across hot coals. You just have to believe in your product, service, or idea and know that it helps people do things better, smarter, safer, at less cost, with less effort, in less time. You must have no doubt that you offer value. So the first secret to expecting "yes" is not a secret at all.

Become Aware of Any Negative Thoughts and Replace Them with Positive Thinking

Let's say you harbor some negative thoughts that keep you from wanting to make cold calls. Maybe you feel like you're disturbing prospects from something more important, or that your call is simply an annoyance. The next secret is to purposefully quash those negative thoughts by replacing them with more positive thinking.

With a master's degree in counseling, I've run into more than a few people who walk around, unaware, that they're filling their heads with negative images. We'll talk more about this in Chapter 7. But since cold calling is a type of sales presentation—as is every conversation you have with your prospects and customers—the tips are important here, too.

When you hear yourself saying, "They'll never agree to this," or "I hope they don't answer," or "One more person to bother," eliminate those thoughts by replacing them with something else. Here are some ideas to think about:

- Picture your customers enjoying the benefits of your product. Keep photos or testimonials from satisfied clients, and when you're hesitant to make the next call, look at them. No one sends you letters? The next time you talk with a satisfied customer, write down his complimentary words.
- See yourself enjoying the benefits of selling the product. Think of how you and your family benefit—or will benefit—from your sales ability. Keep a photo on your desktop of the vacation you enjoyed because of your hard

work. See yourself enjoying the fruits of your labor instead of visualizing yourself "bothering" someone in the middle of the workday.

- Consider this: Nothing ventured, nothing gained. If you talk yourself out of making the calls, you have no chance to make the sale. When you pick up the phone, you create the opportunity to sell something that helps someone.

AFFIRM THE POSITIVE. My dad frequently played a song called "Ac-cent-tchu-ate the Positive," which was recorded by Bing Crosby and nominated for an Academy Award. The lyrics start out with the song title, then go on to say, "Eliminate the negative, Latch on to the affirmative." How that advice seeped into my soul!

Is it corny? You bet. True? Absolutely. Become aware of the way you see things, because when you look at them in a positive light, the things you look at change. In fact, adopting a positive, "expect yes" mentality is the foundation for mastering the multistep cold-calling process. Once you have the vision, you can make the calls.

DETERMINE THE RESULT YOU WANT FROM THE CALL

Pinning down what you want from your cold call is critical to its success. Many salespeople think they want to make a sale, and this is the true objective for some. If you have a simple transactional sale like a magazine subscription, a fundraising drive, or a snow removal service, you can close the sale in one conversation with a persuasive pitch.

The majority of sales, however, require higher trust on

the part of the buyer. In those cases, the point of the cold call is not to sell, but to see if the prospect has a need, and if so, the goal may be to persuade her to meet with you, visit your website, participate in an informational webinar, schedule a site visit, or test out the product to see if your offer satisfies her need.

Being clear on what constitutes a successful call outcome is important because it's possible, and easier, to settle for less than you should. By establishing your call objective, you won't sell yourself short by being content with just sending collateral, when what you wanted to sell was a face-to-face meeting to discuss needs. Knowing what you want from your time on the phone is the first step toward creating the most effective approach for your call.

PREPARE RELEVANT QUESTIONS TO KEEP THE PROSPECT ENGAGED

Meaningful questions keep your approach from being simply a one-way monologue. For your prospect to truly consider your offer, and for you to know if you should even present your offer, you both need to participate in the sales conversation, asking and responding to each other's questions. If you find that you're doing all the talking, and you haven't checked in to see if you're on the right track for the other person, it's possible that you may be dumping data in to a phone that's being held away from the receiver's ear!

Ideally, the questions you ask will pique a prospect's interest enough to make him want to learn more. Questions that revolve around your processes, presuppose acceptance of your ideas, or are intended to push prospects into saying yes are not meaningful to them, and are likely to get them to shut down and hang up. Instead, pose thoughtful questions that will help you and your buyer discover if there is a need or desire for your product, service, or idea.

Ask only those questions that you really want answered, and are appropriate to ask a stranger. Why, for instance, would someone who doesn't know you want to tell you how she is today? Mistakenly, some salespeople believe this is "rapport building." It isn't. You stand a far superior chance of building rapport (which actually means to be in agreement or alignment) with your prospect when you immediately state your point and help her see why she should care. Avoid asking questions such as:

- Is this a good time to talk? (You have no room to maneuver if they say no.)
- How's your day going so far?
- How are you doing today? (Or, How ya doin'?)
- Is it raining over there yet?

Ask yourself: What information is vital to know from this prospect before I can present my solution or suggest we talk further? Just as a doctor must know if it hurts when you laugh (could be appendicitis!), you also need a certain set of information before you can provide your diagnosis for someone's pain or situation.

Be prepared to ask questions throughout the phone call to create a two-way conversation and not just an information drop. Often, however, salespeople do not ask questions because they immediately detect resistance in their prospect's voice. This wariness tends to occur when prospects aren't presented with an immediate, relevant reason to listen to you. To avoid this, get to your point and why it should matter to them right away.

We'll go into more depth about the approach in just a moment. For now, here is an example to help you see how and where you might ask your first question:

> **YOU: Ms. Kennedy, this is Quiona Smith with Barbarian Architects calling. I'm an architect specializing in Southwestern-style luxury homes, and one of your neighbors, Valerie Maritess, mentioned that you purchased a lot in the area . . . If you've selected your architect already, I certainly don't want to waste your time. Are you still interviewing architects?**

Practice your questions with the answers you're seeking in mind. That way, even if you've been given a prepared script, you can rephrase the questions in words that are comfortable for you. Also, when you're comfortable with your questions, you can give your prospects' answers the attention they deserve to best learn how you can help them.

PLAN YOUR APPROACH, PITCH, AND CLOSING STEP

The Approach

The first few words of the call are the most challenging. Because you aren't a friend (yet), it's a mistake to pretend you are. Did you notice that Quiona didn't ask, "How are you today?" as a friend would have the right to, after she stated her name? Quiona moved directly to her point and why her prospect might sincerely care about the call.

Start by giving the prospect the information she needs to determine if she wants to listen to you. Provide your name and company, and either how you're connected to her (and by implication, how she's connected to you), how you found her name, or why you're calling her.

Imagine that your prospect picks up the ringing phone while simultaneously checking her email. Because she is polite, and always open to new ideas, she listens—well, half listens—to your name, wondering to herself, "Do I know him?" Answer that question immediately by providing a bridge between who you are and why it could matter to her. Provide the connection she needs to continue listening by succinctly explaining one of the following:

- How you know her
- Who referred you
- Where you met her
- What you have in common
- Where you read her name
- Which tradeshow you both attended
- Which group you both belong to
- Any other touch point that gives her the idea that you may know enough about her needs that her time can be well spent talking to you

Here's how you might say it:

- Hi, Ted. This is Buster Brown with Cute Pups. Sophie Henson suggested I phone you . . .
- Hi, Alice. This is Brady Champers calling from Shmendrical's Bed and Breakfast. Because we're both members of Meeting Professionals International, I thought . . .

- Hi, Mr. Johns. This is Erica Lia with EL&V Air Conditioners. Your neighbors use our service and they thought you might also like working with honest, reliable, clean air-conditioner service folks! *(If you can mention the neighbors' names, this will be still more powerful and persuasive.)*

Omitting this link is a significant oversight. So is asking your prospect to do your work for you. Notice how these next all-too-familiar approaches provide no connecting touchpoint. They're also the antithesis of the customer-centric approach that is so critical to sales success. The following examples get only to the caller's selling motive. There is no explanation of who the caller is, and no link to help the prospect understand why he may want to listen:

- Hi, is this Mr. Bill Michaels? I'm just calling to ask if you have a need for XYZ services . . .
- Hi, this is Michelle Johnson. I'm calling to find out what you're looking for in a . . .
- Hi, the reason I'm calling today is to see if you might consider . . .

The Pitch

The straightforward, customer-centric approach allows you to create a link to your prospect within a few seconds. Once you establish this connection, briefly talk about your product and how it would be helpful to her, being as specific as possible. Your prospect is still a bit skeptical. If you employ overused, outdated, and meaningless phrases—common "sales speak"—you'll play right into that skepticism. Your pitch should explain your product's strongest benefits and features so that your ability to help the prospect is immediately clear.

Example:

> **YOU: Good morning, Ms. Coore. This is Maya Ashley with High Impact Presentations. I read in the *Arizona Republic* that you'll be holding your annual conference in Phoenix. We offer prominent business improvement speakers who are located in the area so that you can schedule top speakers at your meeting, at a reduced fee. Are you still looking for a few top-notch business speakers for your educational workshops?**

Or:

> **YOU: Hi, Ms. Guttierez. This is Connie Richards with Bestest Insurance Company. Parker Daniel suggested I phone you to see when you'll be reviewing your company's benefit plans. Parker and I have been working together for almost five years, and he says his company has saved thousands on premiums since working with us, and they're able to offer the most competitive benefits package. Do you review benefits in September like Parker's company?**

Look back to the questions you already prepared and incorporate them into the end of your pitch to help move the sales conversation toward the close.

The Closing Steps

The questions you ask throughout the call will help you learn about a prospect's need for your product, and let you fully understand if what you offer can help her. If your prospect does express interest, the next step, asking for your call objective—the sale, the appointment, approval to send collateral—flows comfortably and logically.

Back to Maya and Connie.

When your call objective is to send collateral and schedule a follow-up call:

> **YOU: Good morning, Ms. Coore. This is Maya Ashley with High Impact Presentations. I read in the *Arizona Republic* that you'll be holding your annual conference in Phoenix. We offer prominent business improvement speakers who are located in the area so that you can schedule top speakers at your meeting, at a reduced fee. Are you still looking for a few top-notch business speakers for your educational workshops?**
>
> **PROSPECT: Well, we have almost everyone scheduled. I have been looking for a strong female speaker.**
>
> **YOU [*based on the questions you previously crafted*]: We have some very strong women here. Do you have a specific topic in mind?**

Then, after a thorough conversation about her needs and how you can help her:

> **YOU: How about if I send you a link to her website? You can watch a short video of her, and I'll follow up with you. When would you like me to call you to see if she's what you're looking for?**

Or when your objective is to set up a meeting:

YOU: Hi, Ms. Guttierez. This is Connie Richards with Bestest Insurance Company. Parker Daniel suggested I phone you to see when you'll be reviewing your company's benefit plans. Parker and I have been working together for almost five years, and he says his company has saved thousands on premiums since working with us, and they're able to offer the most competitive benefits package. Do you review benefits in September like Parker's company?

PROSPECT: Yes, we do.

YOU: I see and . . . [*At this point you and she might have additional questions for each other.*] Well, to determine if we can offer you a better rate and plan, it would be important to conduct a confidential audit. That's how we started with Parker's group, too. Before that, it would be helpful to meet so that you can review the possible options to see if we have plans that are a fit for your company's unique needs. So, would you have time this week, or next week, Monday, Wednesday, or Thursday, to meet?

When it's a transactional sale:

YOU: Good morning, Ms. Fishel. This is Pablo Spaniela with Top Tree Trimmers. We're working in your neighborhood next week, and if you have trees with limbs that are dangerously close to power lines or your walkway, we can safely cut those down, and take care of the trees, at a very reasonable cost. Do you have any tree limbs that are worrying you? [*Wait for response. Then, your response.*] Oh. Absolutely. We can take care of those for you before someone gets hurt. We'll be in your neighborhood

Monday and Tuesday. Do you have a preference? Let's see on Monday, I have 11 a.m., 3 p.m. and 4:30 p.m., open right now, and Tuesday, it's noon or later. Which works best for you? Great. Tuesday at 1 p.m. Perfect. We'll confirm this in an email to you, if you'd like. And your email address is ... Great. We'll see you Tuesday. Oh, and if you have any neighbors who are also concerned, if you'd let them know about us ...

Always Plan to Ask for the Next Step

The scenarios that we've looked at ended in forward movement because, in each case, the prospect expressed interest. Because this is not always how it works (oh, if only!), it's up to you to set the stage for your next contact with her before getting off the phone.

Let's say that you're an independent meeting planner, working with large companies who plan corporate events. Your call objective is to set up an appointment with the director of sales to discuss how you can design a meeting with significant return on investment. You call the DOS, introduce yourself, present your pitch, and ask your questions to determine if he might have a need for your services. Your questions uncover the truth: He isn't interested. He is working with a planner, and she is doing a great job. Frankly, he says, he had never seen his team so pumped as their last meeting. Of course, you thank him and then, before completing the call, set the stage for the next contact. In that way, when you call back, you're no longer cold calling, but following up *as promised*.

Always ask the prospect for a commitment to a next step, or provide a commitment to him, even if he isn't presently interested in your product or service. For example:

PROSPECT: Thank you, but we're in the first year of a three-year contract we negotiated with Sheila Norita. She is doing a great job for us, maybe you know her, so no, we really aren't interested.

YOU: Thank you. So, may I ask you, is Sheila doing all your meetings, including the smaller ones?

PROSPECT: Yup.

YOU: You must be pleased with her! Okay, because things sometimes change, may I stay in touch with you, call you again in nine months, let's say?

PROSPECT: Sure, if you want.

YOU: Thank you. I'll email you from time-to-time so you'll remember me, and I'll call you in May.

PROSPECT: Fine.

Next year, May:

YOU: Hi, Mr. Goldstein. This is Tiffany Poodle from Poodle Meeting Strategies. As promised, I'm following up on our conversation last August about your needs for a corporate meeting planner. Do you have any meetings that are in need of some pizzazz, within budget?

PROSPECT: As a matter of fact, we've been working with Sheila Norita, but she just told me during our annual convention that she's expecting and will be away on maternity leave most of this year . . .

While following up with uninterested prospects obviously won't always lead to a sale so seamlessly, it's important to keep in mind that situations can change. Even if a prospect is entirely pleased with his situation when you first introduce yourself, always try to get a commitment for a follow-up to keep the door open for future sales. This way, the next time you call, you may be speaking with both a qualified buyer and a REAL one.

FIND REAL PROSPECTS

Now that you have the process for creating an exceptional cold call, you can further enhance your sales results by selling to REAL prospects. REAL prospects are different from *qualified* prospects.

A REAL prospect is:

Ready to buy
Eager for the outcome your product/service/idea offers
At this time, interested
Listening with a desire to buy a product like yours

A qualified prospect *theoretically* could purchase your product. If you sell mortgage services, a *qualified* prospect is anyone who owns a home. A REAL prospect, however, is a homeowner who either:

- Needs money for other things and refinancing is an option to get that money,
- Wants to save money by reducing interest payments through the better rate that you offer, or
- May have a need for a new mortgage because he is moving to a new home.

If you try to sell your mortgage services to a homeowner with an interest rate lower than what you can offer and with no desire to get money from her home, you might as well just hit your head against the wall. You're not going to make the sale even though the homeowner is a *qualified* prospect. She may have had a need for a mortgage service company three years ago when she purchased her home. She also may have a need for what you offer in the future. Right now, however, she needs you about as much as Arizona needs more heat in the summertime. Not at all.

Make cold calls to REAL prospects and you'll experience less frustration and enjoy more sales. Of course, the only way to know if they're REAL is to pick up the phone and question them to see if they have a need. Asking the prepared questions we discussed earlier in this chapter will help you distinguish REAL prospects from qualified ones.

The distinction here is how you feel about yourself at the end of the day. If your goal is to set an appointment with five out of the fifty leads you call each day, and you only manage to set one, it may be simply because your list was qualified, but your prospects weren't REAL. When you talk to fifty REAL prospects, and you apply the structures we've discussed, you can expect to meet your quota—and then some.

When a prospect shows interest but may not be ready to buy right now, remember to establish the next follow-up date. If he's qualified but not REAL, disengage quickly and politely. Move to the next person on the list to see if he's REAL so you can help him save money, increase productivity, etc. Some straightforward ways to disengage are:

- Thank you. Do I have your approval to follow up with you after the summer? That would be perfect? Excellent! I'll call you in September to set up a meeting to review the concierge services your employees will love!

- Thank you. I appreciate your honesty with me and won't waste your time.
- Thank you for letting me know. If it's okay with you, I'll phone you in another six months to check in. Will that be okay? No? I appreciate knowing that. Thank you.
- You seem very pleased with your current supplier. I won't pester you then. When would it be okay if I followed up with you? Never? Okay. I respect that. Thank you for your time.

As discussed in the previous section, always try to set the stage for a future follow-up in case they might become REAL prospects later. If they're open to speaking with you later, then great—you've landed a lead.

MAKE THE CALL

Schedule a block of time to make your calls, even if it's only fifteen minutes at a time. Then, keep your headset on or the phone in your hand. Stay in "phone mode" and you'll be more likely to stay in the mood. Keep dialing for dollars!

If you really don't enjoy making cold calls, plan them for either first thing in the morning to get them over with, or just before you go to lunch. Like anything else you dislike, if you put it off long enough, there is no time left to do it and you really don't want to miss out on the opportunity for new leads, sales, and profits! Try to schedule the same time each day so that it becomes part of a natural routine.

Finally, when you place the call, remember that the person is judging every nuance to determine if he trusts what you're saying to him. He can't see you and he doesn't know you so he bases his decisions on how you make him feel. Sound pleased to be talking with him, but not over the top! Let him feel your smile, and your excitement for your product and his success.

One of the sweetest things to remember about cold calling is that, at the very worst, all someone can do is hang up. When you prepare for your call, present your message authentically and in a customer-centric manner to give yourself the opportunity to win big.

I think the biggest problem many salespeople have is that they don't handle rejection well. That is the number one reason people can't handle sales. Someone on the other side of the phone gives them a little bit of attitude and they freak out. I have always lived by what my dad taught me, which is the more doors you knock on, the more people that say yes. If they could only realize nothing can happen from someone saying no other than moving on to the next possible sale, they would be much more successful.

—Kory Hershkowitz, author's nephew and
Vice President of Sales, MegaColor Corporation

5

Using Voice Mail to Start and Maintain the Sales Conversation

Practice is just as valuable as a sale. The sale will make you a living; the skill will make you a fortune.
—Jim Rohn

Every sale begins with an introduction. You must, in some fashion, introduce yourself to your future customer. Cold calling prospects, as we saw in Chapter 4, can be a very successful way to make that introduction. But the challenge with the phone (as if cold calling isn't challenging enough) is to actually get to speak—live and in person!—with the prospect. With caller ID, and hectic schedules, connecting for even a few minutes to discuss a prospect's existing situation and upcoming needs can be a struggle.

Often, you're left with no choice but to leave a voice message. When that happens, your caller—who doesn't even know you—makes a split-second decision to listen to your message or not, and then, just as quickly, decides whether to jot down your number, or just hit Delete. That's a lot of pressure riding on your message!

The good news is that the opportunity to directly connect with your prospect when she's not available exists at all. Not that long ago, voice mail wasn't an option. Now, it's up to you to make it worth listening to.

Crafting voice messages that heighten the chance that your prospect will be interested enough to return your call, and creating outgoing voice messages that sell for you in your absence, is what this chapter is about.

CREATE MESSAGES THEY WANT TO RETURN

Crafting a message your prospect wants to return starts with understanding your call purpose. Too often salespeople leave a full-blown sales presentation as a voice message. It's rarely productive to think, "This may be my only chance to connect with him so I'll tell him everything." Creating a compelling voice mail message is like developing a winning cold call script—but on steroids! Like the cold call, you need to have a clear objective; unlike it, that goal can't be to sell or get the appointment. With voice mail, you can plan on accomplishing only one thing: generating enough interest so that the prospect will either return your call or accept your next one.

If you're confident that your prospect isn't going to be available, you can have your voice mail script ready to use. Of course, that's pretty much impossible to know, so always be prepared to either speak directly to your prospect or leave a message. Some successful salespeople purposefully make their cold calls before or after normal work hours, hopeful that their first attempt will result in a voice mail message. Their purpose is to leave a quick message for the prospect so the next time they call, as they say they will, during standard hours, their name is recognized. ("Hi, Mary Jo. This is Fred with StageHands. I'll call you back later tomorrow. Sorry I missed you.") This strategy can work, because the second call is a "warmer" call. But even then you must be prepared for a live person answering the phone, even at 5 a.m. With call forwarding, mobile phones, constant travel, and the frequent desire to get to work early or stay late (to not be disturbed!), it's possible to connect at any hour.

Formulating an effective voice mail script follows the same basic pattern as that of composing the cold call script. The four steps to creating a persuasive voice mail are:

1. Introduce yourself.
2. Create a bridge to your buyer.
3. Pitch with a meaningful benefit.
4. Ask for or tell her the next action step.

1. Introduce Yourself

The natural first step when leaving a voice mail is to introduce yourself. Provide only your name and the organization you represent. Do not give any additional information because you have not yet created a desire for the other person to listen to you. Anything else you say about yourself, including your title, is superfluous at this point.

2. Create a Bridge to Your Buyer

As with the live cold call, explaining how you're connected to your prospect after you've introduced yourself is essential. This step is even more important in a voice mail message than it is in conversation. Unlike a cold call, when you and your prospect are engaging in a back-and-forth dialogue, there is no sense of a social obligation to listen to a voice message. He can disconnect at will without having to worry about being polite.

Simply mention the same connection you planned to provide if you had the chance to speak with a live person. Example:

Let's say you restore vintage collector cars and you're calling a list of owners who recently purchased cars at a car auction. To achieve your message goal, you'll need to develop a bridge or connection interesting enough to make your buyer want to return your call, or accept your next call. The strongest link, because you haven't met and only have his name as a result of buying the auction list, is your love of collector cars (assuming that you do love them).

YOU: Hi, Ron. This is David Weiner with Collection Restoration. Like you, I love vintage automobiles . . .

If you don't love cars (or whatever else it is you sell), it's important to find an alternate way to make a connection. If your list provides other data, focus on that. Start with common ground, and the more significant you can make the connection, the better your results will be.

YOU: Hi, Ron. This is David Weiner with Collection Restoration. I see you just purchased a 1953 powder blue Corvette at the Barrett Jackson auction. That car is amazing! [*Again, you must mean this!*] Or: Powder blue was the prettiest color they used that year. Or: I can still remember seeing those beauties on the road! Or: Their beauty is so classic.

All options, like everything else we've talked about, rest on honesty:

YOU: Hi, Ron. This is David Weiner with Collection Restoration. I'm not sure if it's appropriate for us to talk. We work with owners of vintage cars to help them . . . Is this something you're considering for that Corvette you bought at the auction?

You can also try a lighthearted approach:

YOU: Hi, Ron. This is David Weiner with Collection Restoration. You are one lucky man to have walked away with that 1953 powder blue baby. I heard the bidding was extreme.

Selling services or products that may be necessary, but uncomfortable to talk about, creates additional challenges. Is it possible to leave a voice mail for a stranger and expect her to call you back when she doesn't want to think about or admit a need for what you offer? Honesty, directness, and a touchpoint all help to motivate her.

If you sell pre-need funeral services, for instance, what can you say to persuade someone to talk to you? Convincing her to return your call takes sensitivity and some imagination.

YOU: Hello, Mrs. White. This is Stefanie Song with All You Need. This may not be an appropriate time for us to talk, but as a member of the Class of 1940, you're being offered . . .

Or:

Hello, Mrs. White. This is Stefanie Song from All You Need. Because you attended the Good Livin' Health Fair last month, my guess is that you want to take good care of yourself and those around you. One way to do that is to prepare for the future, today . . .

Some people, based on either personal experience or negative stereotypes, believe that sales folks don't know how to tell the truth. When you say something like, "This may not be an appropriate time to talk," or "You may not want to think about this now," your credibility skyrockets. If you've been taught to sell in a manipulative manner, this advice will seem counterintuitive. In fact, as we've previously discussed, by stepping back and talking frankly about the elephant in the room, you immediately let your prospect know that you can be trusted, and that his or her best interest is more important than pushing the sale.

---

3. Pitch with a Meaningful Benefit

Starting your voice message with a connection or common ground defrosts the call and presents you as a professional. The next step is to introduce the reasons your prospect might want to buy your product: your pitch. When your link to the prospect is weak, but you're confident your product's benefit will be compelling, you can successfully follow your introduction with your pitch without mentioning a connection to her. Focus on benefits instead of product features because your customer's success—not the features of your product—is the center of the buying process.

These examples don't offer a link; instead, they pop out of the box with a benefit-driven pitch.

Hello, Mrs. White. This is Stefanie Song from All You Need. We can help you save money for your children and make their lives so much more comfortable when the time comes. I know this is something you may not want to talk about right now, but you have the ability to ease their burden, without spending a penny today. If you aren't aware of pre-need services, this is a good time to talk so you can spare them . . . (*In this one, the benefit is the focus on the children.*)

Additional examples:

Hi, Abby. This is Lily Kate with Megacolor Printing. You can attract more people to your trade show booth at your next trade show and save money in the process. We can help you . . .

Hi, Melinda. This is Dena Tatum from Mom's Inc. Throwing a birthday party that is child-friendly, different, fun, and within a reasonable budget seems impossible these days. We specialize in doing just that . . .

A major difference between crafting your pitch for a voice mail message and a cold call is brevity. As important as it is to state your benefits concisely when *speaking* with the buyer, it's invaluable in the voice message. A good way to think of the voice mail pitch is as an abridged version of the cold call pitch.

BOOST CUSTOMER-CENTRICITY. No sales conversation should include information that doesn't matter to the other person, and most especially a cold call voice mail. Without a robust focus on what is crucial to his success, he just won't continue to listen to the recording you leave.

The next logical question is: How do you know what matters to someone when you haven't even spoken to him? Often your call list provides all the information you need. When you truly have no way to know what matters to a prospect, pitch the fundamental, generic reason most people enjoy your goods or solution.

You can always do a quick Internet search to learn more about customers, and this is sometimes a good idea. Practically, however, researching every business or consumer you call may not be a smart use of time.

BENEFITS AND FEATURES. Salespeople must sell the benefits of their product or service before they support them with features because the benefit is what matters to the buyer. Benefits are the intangible things customers enjoy as a result of a product's or service's features. Features are the tangible aspects of the product itself.

It amazes me how often salespeople believe they're selling benefits (which is what they *should* be selling) when they're relying on product features to persuade the buyer. If you sell hotel space, a feature may be your great location. The benefit of that location could be the *convenience* to dining, mass transportation, or the home office. Other benefits of the location feature may be *reducing stress, saving time, saving money* on transportation costs. Sell benefits. After your prospect sees what is in it for him or her, then you can back up your benefit promises with the features that will make those benefits happen. Here are other examples of benefits supported by features:

Examples:

- You'll increase profits and contacts (benefit) by attending this year's annual meeting (feature).
- Keeping your hair shiny and soft (benefit) is exactly what a home water softener can do (feature) . . .
- Being certain that you're comfortable, and that your back is properly aligned (benefits), is the basis for how our GoodBack chairs are constructed (feature).

4. Ask for or Tell Her the Next Action Step

The last step gets you to your message objective: asking for the return call or telling the prospect what you'll do next. Be specific and direct. Once you clearly explain the next step, remind him one more time of a benefit he stands to gain by talking with you.

Examples:

Hi, Ron. This is David Weiner with Collection Restoration. Like you, I love vintage automobiles, and we work with owners of collector cars, like the 1953 Corvette you recently purchased, to help them get every bit of enjoyment out of their cars. We restore them to perfection so they drive the way they should and look as sweet as they are. If this is something you're interested in, please call me at 555-555-5555. Again, that was 555-555-5555. Whether you plan to drive that car or double your investment, I can help you. Talk to you soon.

Hello, Mrs. White. This is Stefanie Song with All You Need. This may not be an appropriate time for us to talk, but as a member of the Class of 1940, you're being

offered a very special way to make your children's life less stressful and help them save money, too. We fairly and sensitively offer final pre-need arrangements. This may not be something you're excited to talk about right now, but I promise you it makes everything easier to bear for your loved ones. I'll phone you back next Wednesday to talk about how this service can benefit your family. Of course, if you'd like to make an appointment to visit us, my name is Stefanie and the phone number is 555-555-5555. Again, that's 555-555-5555. You'll be helping your family get through the hardest part of their lives.

Hi, Abby. This is Lily Kate with Megacolor Printing. If you'd like to attract more people to your booth at your next trade show and save money, too, we can help you by providing high-quality sell sheets that your buyers won't toss before they leave the show floor. High Impact Presentations increased sales 11 percent when they started using our services and we can do that for you, too. Please call me at 800-555-5555. [*Then repeat.*] I'll phone you again, too, so we can talk about increasing your sales and profits.

TIPS TO ENHANCE COLD-CALLING SUCCESS

Small details can have a huge impact on your buyer when leaving a cold voice mail message. The following little-known strategies build on your aim to help your buyer create greater success. Use these tips to differentiate your messages from those of your competition.

Help Them Opt Out and Say No!

Just as you wouldn't spam your buyers with unwanted emails, you don't want to spam them with your phone messages. One way of letting them know that you respect their wishes is to let them opt out of receiving additional sales calls from you:

> If, for whatever reason, you would prefer *not* to hear back from me, please leave me a voice mail message or send an email to Marketing@TimRichardson.com and I'll respect your wishes. Again, the toll free number here is at 800-555-5555.

> I understand that the machinery you're currently using may be producing at a rate and price that work for you. If that's the case, I don't want to waste your time. If you do not wish to receive follow-up materials from me, I'm happy to honor your request. My phone number is . . . or if you prefer, my email address is . . . If I don't hear from you, I'll plan to phone you next quarter to talk about the two-person dozer that is just now on the drawing board.

> I'll follow up this message with an email, and if you'd prefer that I not send additional messages, please let me know and we will not contact you further.

There is a fine line between being persistent and being annoying. The last thing you want to do is be a pest. Some people need to be contacted five to seven times before they pay attention (maybe because over the years, we salespeople have trained our prospects that they shouldn't worry—we'll be back!). But giving them the option of opting out so they aren't "hounded" is a respectful approach that might convince them that you're worth talking to! Additionally, this is an easy way to discover if they are REAL prospects or simply qualified.

Never Skip the Follow-Up

With database systems today, it's easy to schedule follow-up calls. After every cold call or voice message, create a new "to-do." Even if you asked your prospect to get back to you, take control of the sale. Operating under the misguided thinking that "oh, if they want me, they'll get back to me" limits potential. The follow-up call may take place in seven days, seven months, or seventeen months, but put it on the calendar!

If you haven't been following up the voice messages you leave, do it now. You may find it more profitable to follow up and call the prospects who never returned your calls before reaching out to others. Even if they have only the slightest recall of your name, company name, or the benefit you suggested, the call is no longer officially a cold call, but a defrosted one!

ALWAYS SAY IMPORTANT INFORMATION AGAIN. It doesn't matter if you've left seven previous messages, or even if you have a long-term relationship with your customer. Do him the favor of leaving your full name and phone number every time you call. Don't force him to replay your message to figure out if you're Sue H. from the Scottsdale office or Sue P. from Houston. Repeat your phone number at least twice and say it *slowly and clearly* so he'll be able to memorize it long enough to call you back while on the go. "Little" courtesies can get big results—like a returned call!

Consider saying your phone number initially and again at the close of the message. In that way, if they recognize you, they won't have to listen through the entire message.

Have More Than One Voice Mail Message Prepared and Ready

As discussed earlier, providing an opt-out is one way to avoid bothering uninterested prospects. However, if you find yourself leaving voice mails that go unanswered, it's possible that you may have called at an inopportune time, and as intrigued as a prospect was in what you said, he had no time to follow up with you. Or maybe you selected the wrong benefit to highlight in your message, even though it's a factor that the majority of your existing customers really appreciate. Planning a series of voice mail messages gives you new opportunities to pique a prospect's interest by positioning your benefits differently each time. If you'd like, you can include an opt-out after each one to give uninterested prospects the chance to be left alone.

Jim Pancero, sales trainer and author of *You Can Always Sell More*, recommends creating ten unique voice mail messages to leave for prospects. Each message offers a fresh benefit and a new way to look at those benefits. He numbers each message and makes a note in his database so he doesn't leave the same message twice. Creating ten messages may be over the top for you, so start with a series of at least five distinct messages. Return to your list of benefits to create these concise sales pitches.

Here are ideas for you to consider:

Sample Cold Call 1

Hi, Zach. This is Phil Goldberg with Champion Products. Bob Morrison gave me your name. I created a sales mastery program for Bob's department that increased his sales 22 percent. If that's something that might interest you, let's talk about the challenges your team may be experiencing since your merger. My phone number is 555-555-5555. Again, that's Phil Goldberg, 555-555-5555, and we'll only need about twenty minutes to see if this mastery program can give your team the edge.

Sample Cold Call 2

Hi, Zach. This is Phil Goldberg with Champion Products. If you're interested in increasing the effectiveness of your newly merged sales team, I'd be honored to talk with you about how you can generate additional profit and drive revenue without adding new sales folks. If you'd like to set up a fifteen-minute exploratory call, I'm in the office Monday through Thursday this week. My phone number is 555-555-5555. Again, that's Phil Goldberg, 555-555-5555, and the purpose is to help you increase revenue without adding to your existing sales team.

Sample Cold Call 3

Hi, Zach. This is Phil Goldberg, 555-555-5555, with Champion Products. Based on my research, your organization has undergone three mergers in eighteen months. Maintaining a high-functioning sales team during times of change is stressful at best. I can make your life easier by helping you create a new sales culture that embodies the best of each company's sales structures. I'll phone you back next month when things settle down a bit for you, and if you'd like to call me sooner, my number is . . .

Somewhere around the eighth time Jim leaves a message, he playfully says: *Hi, this is Jim Pancero. I'm not going away because I know I can increase your sales by at least 15 percent. Please call me at 555-555-5555.* Jim says that his prospects laugh and tend to call him back. At this point they believe him on both claims!

Treat each call as a new call rather than as a follow-up. Saying "Hi, I'm following up on the call I left for you last month" is likely to back-fire because it focuses on you and not your customer's needs.

LEAVE APPROPRIATE TIME BETWEEN CONTACTS. The reality is that eventually Jim does go away if a prospect doesn't call back. No one does business with a pest even if she respects persistence. Unless the deal is time sensitive and the offer will disappear at the end of the week, leave at least one week between calls. Calling more often not only makes you look revenue desperate, it's also obnoxious. A good calling schedule is:

Call 1. January, week 1
Call 2. January, week 3
Call 3. February, week 3
Call 4. March, week 3
Call 5. May, week 3
Call 6. July, week 3
Call 7. November, week 3
Call 8. March, following year

Call 9. November, following year
Call 10. June, year after

Of course, you can substitute the phone calls with follow-up emails or handwritten notes. We'll talk more about selling in writing in later chapters. But the ideal is to connect in real time with the prospect to begin a sales conversation in earnest.

When a Prospect Won't Return Your Call

If someone doesn't want to talk to you or buy from you, no matter how often you call her, she won't. In these cases, you'll need to use your best judgment and figure out when it's time simply to stop calling. However, if you've already had the opportunity to speak to someone at least once and she won't respond to any of your follow-ups, it may be difficult to figure out where to go from there. This is an all-too-common sales experience. You left a cold call message and she called you back. She sounded interested, so you sent her collateral or maybe even a proposal. But when you called to follow up, she stopped taking your calls. This often happens because we are so eager to sell and move forward that we don't take the time to ask enough questions to see if she really needs our solutions.

When you have nothing to lose and you've already left several messages, before giving up, leave a message asking if you've messed up! This may seem rude, and could come across as such if said in anger. A central theme of this book is respect for your customers and seeing the situation from their viewpoint. Both of those behaviors are crucial to incorporate when using this approach:

Hi, Barbara. This is Junie Bell. I've left several messages regarding the imprinted candles you expressed interest in at the Expo!Expo! trade show last June. I don't know if I've done something wrong, or if this is something that you are no longer interested in offering your clients to thank them for their business. You would do me a huge favor if you'd let me know the status by calling me at 555-555-5555 or sending me an email at JunieB@Candles.com.

If you have done something wrong (like being too aggressive), and she calls you back to tell you, what a gift that will be to help you sell better next time! And if you've done nothing wrong, she is likely to call you back to explain why she hasn't reached out to you. Using this in our office has led to great success.

MAKE YOUR OUTGOING VOICE MESSAGE SELL

The flip side of leaving a voice mail is having one left for you. What someone hears on your outbound phone message is a powerful determiner of whether he'll continue to leave his message or just hang up. When you spend time crafting an irresistible voice mail to leave for him, do yourself a favor and craft one for your outbound voice mail, too. When your prospect phones you back, he is listening for clues to help him determine if you're trustworthy and likable. Put as much energy into creating an outbound phone message as you do when leaving your message for a potential buyer.

Take this test: Become your customer—or better yet, a prospect who is still a stranger to you, but takes the time to return your call—and decide if you would bother leaving a message for you! Another good test is to ask family members or friends to listen to your current outbound message. If they didn't know you, which words would they use to characterize the voice they hear?

POSITIVE VOICE MESSAGE ATTRIBUTES	NEGATIVE VOICE MESSAGE ATTRIBUTES
Enthusiastic	Bored
Confident	Tentative
Clear	Garbled
Friendly	Remote
High energy	Dead
Professional	Cutesy
Welcoming	Annoyed
Timely	Old news

The message you leave on your phone should be updated every time the news changes; if you're in the office, it should say that, and when you aren't, it shouldn't say you're there! If you choose to include today's date, be certain you refresh your message daily. Also, if you'll be out of the office until the twelfth, remember to update the message when you return.

Your message should include:

- A short introduction including your name and company name.
- A specific day, date, or time when you'll return the call.

- A brief selling message that motivates your caller to want to talk with you.

The Short Introduction

Begin your outbound message much the same way as you'd leave the information on someone else's voice mail. Provide your name and company name. If you'd like, you can begin with a courteous thank-you. Sometimes it doesn't add to the quality of the voice message, and often, it will have more significance when it's placed in the middle or the end of the voice message.

- Hi! This is Michael Brady. Thank you for calling Chuckles, Inc.

State When You'll Return the Call

Your voice message is an opportunity to offer good customer service to your prospects and customers. When they call, they should know exactly when their inquiry will be answered. If you're out of the office, let your caller know when you'll return the call. If someone other than you is likely to phone him, tell him whom to expect and why that person is phoning instead of you.

- Nancy will get back to you by the end of the day. I'm in transit and can personally return your call after 7 p.m. Eastern Standard Time, if you prefer.
- If you would like my assistant, Gibson Henry, to call you back today, please let us know. Otherwise, I'll return your call Tuesday, January 13, when I return to the office.

You may not always be able to be specific, but always be as helpful as you can. Saying something like "I'll call you as soon as I return," or "when I return to my desk," isn't much help unless you give a clue about when that is.

ELIMINATE USELESS INFORMATION. Vague details, such as telling your caller that you'll have "limited" access to voice mail, aren't helpful, and can even be taken as inadvertent insults by some callers. My interpretation of that message is: "If you're important, I'll call you back. If not, I'll call you—whenever." Instead, just tell them when you're likely to call them back.

Eliminate vague phrases and replace them with more specific and helpful information:

> **INSTEAD OF: I'll have limited access to voice mail.**
> **SAY: I'll return urgent calls between 12:30 and 12:45 p.m. today. I'm in off-site meetings all day.**

> **INSTEAD OF: I'll be checking my voice mail infrequently.**
> **SAY: I'll return your call as soon as I get back to the office Tuesday morning. I'll be in transit throughout the day to-day. If you require information more promptly, Rachel is happy to help you. Rachel's direct line is 555-555-5555 [*and repeat*].**

Some people distinguish between traveling for business and vacation travel. Explaining that you're on vacation is helpful to your prospect if you're not checking calls. You don't need to explain, however, when you're traveling on business. Your customers expect you to travel on business, so telling them this won't change their expectation that you'll call them back promptly. Only distinguish unusual situations and always stay focused on presenting your message to help the other person:

If you would like a return phone call before I get back from vacation, May 12, please mention this when you leave your message. Patti Press will be answering questions while I'm gone. Her number is 555-555-5555 if you'd prefer to call Patti directly.

Motivate with a Brief Selling Message

Here, finally, is your opportunity to sell! Keep it short and focused. Remember to sound enthusiastic about your words. Think about the pitch you'd leave on your prospect's voice machine and try to condense that message even further.

Here are some additional examples of effective outbound messages:

- Hi, and thanks for calling Boulder Falls Kennel and Day Spa. This is Jamie O'Leary and I'll return all calls before 5 p.m. today. When you're away, come let your dog play!
- Hi, this is Karolyn Harmony with Concierge and Meetings Sources. Thank you for calling. Cleo Klementine is retrieving my messages while I'm in transit. If you'd like me to phone you back instead, I'd be happy to do that when I return on Friday, December 1. Please let Cleo know! Otherwise, you'll hear from her within twenty-four hours of your message. Remember, it's a gift to give your team concierge services!
- Hi, this is Nancy Paulson. I'm on vacation and will return all calls when I return August 24. Thanks for calling Neat Closets. Remember, make it a super Neat day! Talk to you soon!
- Thank you for calling C & C Golf Supplies. Jason and Kevin will return all calls Monday, June 16. Jason's mobile

number is 555-555-5555, if you'd like to talk with him before then. We're looking forward to fitting you to a tee!

Cheesy won't cut it!

You're always selling your reputation. As tempting as it is to leave a flippant message after a long day, don't. Always represent yourself professionally. With so many people working virtually, and no one to help temper our judgment, and because so many salespeople develop such close relationships with customers, it's challenging not to leave a message, once in a while, that sounds something like this:

Hey, today is Monday [but it's Tuesday] and I'm off skiing. Conditions are excellent and life is short. You know I'll get back to you just as soon as I get off the mountain. Wish you were here. At the beep, leave it.

Imagine your friend and client sitting with the CEO and CFO, and she has just pitched your product to them. The CFO has a few questions. They call you on speakerphone and hear that message.

Always be prepared to leave a voice mail message anytime you pick up the phone to make a cold call. Practice and prepare your message to present yourself professionally, directly, and concisely, and always be prepared for the best option: that the person will actually answer the phone. Pay attention to your outgoing message, too. Every communication a prospect hears persuades her to believe in you—or not. Apply the ideas and strategies from this chapter and neither you nor she will be tempted to hang up at the beep again!

PART III

High-Impact Presentations That Sell

Sitting through a boring presentation is like torture. Delivering one is even worse. You watch your buyers' eyes glaze over and you feel the sheer panic setting in. You realize you're talking, maybe even rambling, and you can't "shut up"! You can feel the pit, not just in your stomach, but in your throat, too. Both you and your customers can't wait for the presentation to end.

There's a better way! Even though making a sales presentation can be nerve-racking, you never need be nervous again. Once you change your thinking from what can go wrong to what can go right, and prepare for that success, you'll change your world and your buyers' views, too.

Part III provides the tips, techniques, and strategies you need to create sales presentations that are memorable, interesting, and fun. You'll discover a little-known no-fail formula to structure your presentation to get the results you desire. You'll learn to use both a conclusion and a close to move toward a successful outcome, how to handle Q & A professionally (even when you can't answer their question), and how to present yourself—and your solution—with confidence. In Part III, you'll develop the skills to dramatize and polish every presentation so that your sales results move from average to great and from good to awesome!

6

Structuring the High-Impact Sales Presentation

In classical times when Cicero had finished speaking, the people said, "How well he spoke," but when Demosthenes had finished speaking, they said, "Let us march."
—Adlai Stevenson

All presentations fit into one of three types: ceremonial, informational, and persuasive. This chapter discusses how to structure the only kind of *sales* presentation that exists: the persuasive kind.

Ceremonial presentations aren't necessary to discuss in this book because they're delivered only at life cycle events like weddings, bar mitzvahs, and graduations. You may wonder, though, why there isn't a thorough discussion of informational presentations. The answer is this: because they don't belong in the salesperson's world. An informational presentation delivers impartial and objective data, statistics, and facts through which the listener can make an informed decision. Because you are *paid* to influence—to persuade and sell, not simply inform and tell—this chapter is devoted to helping you structure your data in the most persuasive way possible.

Your sales presentation goal is to make a compelling case so your prospects grasp that you represent the smartest choice for them. That's accomplished best when you help them become aware of their situation as it presently exists, and how much better it will look when they work with you and apply your solutions.

Persuasive presentations follow this basic structure:

1. Open with a compelling argument.
2. Provide your solution.
3. Present your conclusion.
4. Ask for the next step.

OPEN WITH A COMPELLING ARGUMENT

A sales presentation, unlike a cold call, is an expected sales pitch. Whether it's at a tradeshow, a formal meeting, a casual lunch, on a conference call, or in your prospect's office, you both know why you're talking together. You have something he may want to buy and he's ready to hear what you have to say.

At this point, some salespeople believe that their goods sell themselves and that crafting a compelling and persuasive opening won't impact the results they receive. Believing that your customer doesn't need you to set the stage for the solutions you're about to offer is a mistake. When you structure the presentation so that you make it immediately clear that your prospect is harming his bottom line by not using your solutions—your product, service, or idea—you motivate him to buy.

Your opening lays the groundwork, much like an opening argument in a courtroom. Think of yourself as an attorney, speaking to a group of people specially selected to look at what you have to say with impartiality—yet hopeful that the final decision is cast in your favor. Pointedly, show your "jury" that their existing practices or processes are lacking in some way, to win your case.

A well-structured opening creates anticipation for your solution.

An Internet marketing company I work with sells business-to-business advanced software solutions. Their cutting-edge solutions are so far beyond what their prospects currently use, that even though buyers are impressed with what they've developed, they don't see the need to buy the product. They also see the software solutions as an additional cost of business, rather than as a way to drive revenue and save money. If the Internet company simply explains what they have to offer—revolutionary advanced technology— they sell only to those prospects who love the coolest new technology. If, on the other hand, they start the presentation by showing prospects their pain—what they lose each day based on how their current software tracking system works—and then show them how the software takes away that pain, they make a more persuasive case, and more sales.

The sales professionals working with this company might grab the attention of their C-level buyer by structuring their opening argument like this:

Right now, based on my discussions with your team (or my research, etc.), the company loads rates using a tedious, expensive, and time-consuming process. Because of that, it's impossible to use loaded rates as a revenue driver. Companies with the ability to load rates instantaneously, however, increase profits X percent daily. That means significant revenue is being lost every day that loaded rates aren't being used. Of course, this wasn't even possible to do until very recently . . .

The Reverend Mort Utley was schooled as a preacher, but was a world-renowned and much-loved sales trainer. He advised presenters to "get them to sit up and listen" and to focus on "the black of the white and the white of the black—the opposite of what they're expecting." These favorite openings are structured to argue his case, by starting with the "pain":

"'There are no Christians in the world today,' says the *Christian Science Monitor*. "I will disprove that."

"Most people do not get what they want out of life."

Startle your buyers with an extreme statement to "get them to sit up and listen."

Here are some additional examples:

When Montana's governor, Brian Schweitzer, was asked to distill his views on energy conservation into a sixty-second sound bite people could appreciate, he structured his words to start with the pain. His opening argument painted a clear picture of the current problem: "Folks," he said, "we've got a problem. We Americans use 6.5 billions barrels of oil a year. We produce 2.5 billion ourselves. We import 4 billion from the world's worst dictators. We need to stop doing that." In just a very few words, his argument compelled us to listen. He made the pain of our existing situation apparent, before moving on to his solution.

I try to do the same thing, in a more lighthearted manner, when presenting sales training programs on communication skills. Because I know that many of the attendees are there not by choice but by "command performance," I know I need to sell the value of the training to them. Many walk in not even realizing that they could be performing more persuasively. I'll ask a series of questions like, "So, how many of you have ever said anything dumb? How many knew it was dumb while it was coming out of your mouth? How many of you then made it even worse? Today, we'll talk about how to keep that foot out of your mouth—and your prospect's, too!" I bring awareness to the fact that they have a common problem and that we're going to solve it.

Uncovering Their Pain

This opening strategy—beginning by making their pain evident—can only be used when you understand their current reality. The research and analysis phase needed to learn about their situation can take weeks or months depending on the complexity of the sale and is beyond the scope of this book. What's important to remember, though, is that the point of your research is to discover if there is a true match between you and the prospect; to uncover if and how your solutions can help her achieve more. Design your questions to understand the facts as they exist and probe to uncover their needs and expectations. Consider using both clarifying and probing questions.

Clarifying questions don't require much thought to answer because the answers are fact based. Still, they're helpful for you to unearth the reality as it exists. Clarifying questions might be:

> Are you happy with the systems you have in place?
> Was there an issue that came up that the system couldn't address?
> How much time does it typically take now to . . . ?
> Have you seen an increase or decrease in your profit margins over the last three years?
> What is your timing for this project?
> Are there advocates for the existing process?
> Would you like to see improvements in any particular area?

Probing questions require the prospect to consider options and respond thoughtfully. They go beyond yes-no answers and facts. So, if your buyer answered "Somewhat, yes" to your clarifying question, "Are you satisfied with the systems you have in place?" a follow-up probing question might be, "What would have to change for you to be totally satisfied with them?" If you're selling real estate, and you ask your client, "Do you like this home?" and the partners turn to each other and say, "What do you think?" your probing follow-up question might be, "What makes you feel happy about a house?"

A probing question shouldn't "lead the jury" such as, "Don't you think . . ." or "Do you agree that . . ." Here are some other examples of probing questions:

> What do you think might happen if . . . ?
> What is the connection between . . . and . . . ?
> How is this a concern for you?

What else would it be helpful for me to know at this
    point?
Can you describe what that might look like?

You might begin to uncover their pain this way:

YOU (*on the phone prior to the presentation date*): **Thank
you for agreeing to let me present our promotional products to you and your marketing team. Because I want to
use your time well, may I ask you a few questions con-
cerning the markets you sell to? Is that okay?**
PROSPECT: Sure.
**YOU: Based on my preliminary research, I believe that
you sell primarily business-to-business. Is that correct?**
**PROSPECT: Yes, we sell to the consumer market, too, but
it's a minor part of our overall strategy and unfortunately
isn't very profitable for us.**
**YOU: Is that an area you'd like to see become more prof-
itable or is enhancing business-to-business sales more
important?** (*A probing question you might want an answer
to could be:* **What do you think it would take to make it a
more profitable area?** *Or:* **How does your overall strategy
impact . . . ?**)
**PROSPECT: Definitely B-B is most important. Right now, we
only make about 2 percent profits from consumer sales. If
we could increase those profits, that would be ideal, but we
don't want to move away from our core business to do it.**

If the conversation ends there, you have enough information to structure your opening argument to demonstrate
the "pain" that exists. You can start your presentation by
saying:

Today, you're showing a 2 percent profit on your consumer operations. If we could increase that to a 3, 4, or 5 percent profit on your same investment, without moving away from your core business-to-business markets, would that be worth talking about?

Most prospects want you to ask questions so that they're confident that you fully understand their challenges. Of course, the more you know, the easier it will be for you to support your opening with custom-tailored solutions that meet their needs.

GRABBING THEIR ATTENTION WHEN NO RESEARCH OPPORTUNITY EXISTS. There may be times when you're presenting your sales message to a group that is so diverse that their "pains" are all over the board. At other times, you may have to present without the benefit of a discussion prior to your presentation. Grabbing attention then, though a bit more difficult, follows the same ideas previously discussed. Determine what is likely to be the most common "pain" they have and begin by addressing that.

Get Their Attention

Your imagination is the most important tool you can use to craft a compelling opening argument. Think of the creative ways in which you can show your prospects their current reality, whether it's a situation you discovered through preliminary research, or a common pain you expect most of them to have. Get them to sit up straight to listen not just to your opening—a view of their pain—but to your solutions to take away their pain, too. Here are two methods to grab their attention:

- Ask a powerful question to get them thinking about their pain. If your question isn't dramatic enough, ask a series of three questions, building up to the most important, funniest, or most meaningful question:

  - "How much time do you waste using the clumsy stylus that comes with your PDA? Anyone ever drop or lose their stylus? In a meeting with a client? There's a reason they're free!" (Slide could show a well-dressed business person crawling under a desk looking for his stylus.)
  - "How many of you would rather go to the dentist than deliver a presentation? For a root canal? Without anesthesia?"
  - "If you could be guaranteed that no one could breach security here, how much easier would it be to conduct business?"

- Be straightforward. When Steve Jobs took over Apple in 1997, his first words to his new executive team weren't "I'm so glad to be back," or "Thank you for your time today." Reportedly, his first words in his first meeting to his new team were: "Okay, tell me what's wrong with this place." (He then answered his own question.) "It's the products! So what's wrong with the products? The products *suck*! There's no sex in them anymore!" (Ya gotta believe that straightforward approach got some attention!)

Another example of a straightforward approach: You're in debt and we can bail you out. It won't be simple but we can make it as easy as possible.

Opening Words That Drain Power

Structuring your presentation for maximum impact means riveting their attention from the very first words. As tempting as it is to start off with a few courtesies, don't waste those important few seconds with words that are weak, meek, or self-centered. Eliminate these boring and common openings:

- Thank you for your time today.
- It is such a pleasure to be here.
- A funny thing happened to me on my way here . . .
- We only have a short time together today . . .
- I'm going to talk to you today about . . .
- I'm sorry that I'm not a professional speaker . . .
- In a minute, we're going to get started talking about . . . but first I'd like to . . .

PROVIDE YOUR SOLUTION

A hidden benefit to opening your sales presentation with a snapshot of your buyer's pain is the opportunity to showcase your understanding of his situation. You not only "get him to sit up straight" by "arguing" your case through describing the facts as you know them, but you also show your value as a strategist or consultant, and your solution can be offered as such. This positive first impression is important because you're no longer viewed as an outsider trying to "sell" a product; you come to the buyer with a method to fix his specific problem.

Before moving to the solution, however, check in with your decision makers to make sure you're absolutely on track. My mentor, Joe Charbonneau, taught this invaluable concept to me: Stop your monologue and start the conversation by asking questions such as:

- Does this sound like something you'd like to explore further?
- Given your strategic initiatives, is this an appropriate time to talk more about this?
- Am I on target for you?

Even when speaking to a large group of decision makers, say:

- With your permission, then, we'll discuss five ways to . . .

Like everything else in the sales conversation, if these questions are not asked in the spirit of respect and with an authentic desire to earn the customer's approval, they will sound manipulative and cheap. These are not "throwaway" questions designed to get him to say yes, as often occurs in poorly structured cold calls.

These questions show respect for your prospects and motivate them to think about why you're really there. Once they give you permission to carry on—and always wait for an answer to your question, or an affirmative nod of the head—you can move forward with your solution knowing you're moving in the direction in which they're interested.

Getting to the Customer-Centric Solution

Your solution is all about them. This should come as no surprise! The pain (their current situation) that you described in your opening argument is alleviated with the solution you bring to the table.

Because your products are only the means to help them achieve the outcomes they desire, focus this part of the sales conversation on their successful outcomes—not on your products. This distinction is critical to sales success. Emphasizing your solution before showing them how their new reality will look as a result of your solution is a common and costly mistake.

As a hotelier, for example, you might have a ballroom that perfectly accommodates a large wedding. The bride, however, isn't interested in the ballroom per se. She is interested in how elegant, special, sophisticated, or comfortable she and her guests will feel in that ballroom.

The old adage that no one buys a drill because he wants a drill is still true. We buy the drill because we need a hole! Your customers, most likely, don't need your sturdy coffee cups, for instance, but they do need a way to serve coffee so that their customers' fingers don't get burned, while the extra-hot coffee stays hot longer, and so the coffee won't leak on their customers' desk or shoes, even if they take all morning to finish drinking it.

The Internet marketing company that we were looking at earlier in the chapter could talk about how the prospect will drive revenue. Perhaps, after their opening argument, they'd say:

Of course, this wasn't even possible to do until very recently. With your approval, then, I'd like to tell you more. Is that okay? [*Wait for answer and clarification.*] What I'm proposing is a way that you can easily and quickly load rates, change rates, identify which rates are

selling, where you can increase what you're charging, and how you can limit availability of a low rate so that when a certain number of items are sold, the system automatically increases the rate. Implementing any of these changes drive revenues for you.

Only after you describe how their situation will improve do you follow up with a description of how your specific product features enable that improvement to happen. Think of this as the evidence that supports your case. This is the time to provide supporting facts.

The Internet marketing company sales rep might say: The software revolutionizes the way rate is loaded because of X, Y, and Z capabilities. The X contributes power while the Y . . .

Based on the buyer, be prepared to go into depth on your solution details. Certainly, a highly analytical group will require more supporting information than a group filled with expressive and amiable personalities. Confirm that you're providing them the information they need. Be direct and clear:

I have documentation on X and am happy to go into that. I want to respect your time, so would you like further background on X or is the collateral in the proposal sufficient?

Would it be more helpful if I walk you through this more thoroughly?

Is this way too much information or should I continue with this detail?

Don't assume that your customer is as interested in the process behind your solution as you might be. On the other hand, don't presume she isn't. Check in to prevent your presentation from sounding like a data dump or too light weight.

Because your solution flows from the initial pain you described, as well as your check-ins to confirm appropriate direction, depth, and breadth, presenting the solution is often the easiest part of the presentation. Just remember that after you highlight the flaws in the existing situation, you must reconstruct that situation to remedy those flaws before discussing the features of your product, idea, or service solution. Skipping this step—that is, moving from pain to product—can result in a major disconnect for your buyer. She sees the problem and understands the offer, but she doesn't necessarily see the connection, even if it seems perfectly obvious to you.

Example:

Imagine that you sell office supplies and through your research and pre-presentation questioning with the architectural firm of Dalmation & Dots, you learn that their vendor, a local supplier since both Dalmation & Dot started the firm, offers no proactive method of ordering supplies. What this means is that the only way to order supplies is to run out of them.

You might say:

"Picture this. You've stayed up most of the night completing the renderings and written proposal for a client review. Even though they requested this at the last minute, you're happy to oblige this important client. When you complete your work, you download it to your assistant so that he can make bound hard copies and FedEx them to all the principles in the client's organization. You call the assistant on your way to the airport for an appointment in another city, to confirm that they've been shipped to your client's six locations, only to discover that your office ran out of binding materials and front covers, and so the proposal has not yet been shipped. The vendor has been called and will deliver the needed materials later today. [*The pain is convincingly described for them.*]

"Sound familiar? How many times has something like that happened here in the last year? In talking with many of you, and your support staff, while I was preparing for this presentation, you told me that the value of being able to depend on supplies being available is, as two of you actually said, 'priceless.' You said that you don't have time to wait once it's discovered that important supplies have run out. Some of you are so concerned about the system that you actually lose productive work time checking on supplies and hoarding them in your offices. What would the financial impact be for you if supplies were ordered automatically? (*Further confirmation that they should sit up and listen; probing question to check in.*)

"The solution we offer is similar to the new minibars in hotels. Just like those, as soon as product is used, it's automatically replaced within twenty-four hours, unless you tell us you need it more quickly. You never need to think about the ordering process again. (*Solution fixes pain.*)

"With your approval, I'll explain more about the automatic system, unless you'd prefer to open the floor to questions . . ."

The entire presentation revolves around the customer. Did you notice how infrequently the word "I" is used, replaced by "you" and "your"? Using the word "I" is fine as long as what you're about to tell them matters to them. If you find yourself saying, "I think, I suggest," or "I'd like" more often that you say, "This is what this means to you, you'll improve profits by," and "this is how you benefit," you may be presenting from an ego-centric rather than customer-centric mode.

PRESENT YOUR CONCLUSION

Structure your next step, the concluding argument, to succinctly bring together the reasons why the prospective client should want to work with you and your company. This is your time to drive home the answer to their most important question, "Out of all the known possibilities, is this the best offer for me and my company?"

Your sales presentation isn't over until you ask for the next step—"the close" that we'll get to in a moment. The conclusion, prior to the close, is vital because it connects your points, helps the decision makers remember them, and persuades them that you can help them. Essentially, you remind them what you told them and add an anchor—an emotional appeal, example, or story—that brings everything together.

When designing your conclusion, ask yourself:

- What points are important for this client to remember even if they recall nothing else?
- If they have to sell this to someone else, what do I want them to say?
- How can I tie this together so they remember it with positive emotion?

I've had the opportunity to view many sales presentations. One of the most common faults I've witnessed time and again is ending prematurely. The saddest part is that this usually occurs when the product is really terrific. Because it's such an awesome solution or offers such terrific value, the salesperson erroneously believes that she doesn't need to ask for the sale, or the next step. She believes the solution sells itself. The salesperson presents her opening argument, follows it with how things will look—the benefits to the prospect of using her product—and explains the product features. Then, and this is the unfortunate part, she stops being persuasive. She asks, "Are there any questions?" Hearing none (and not really expecting any because the product is so good), she says something like, "Okay, well then, thank you, ladies and gentlemen. I appreciate your time," packs up her computer, and exits the meeting. She fully expects to receive a call the next day, or to call them later in the week, hearing that she got the business, and is crushed when they go with her competition.

You may be confident that you've presented the features of your solution to the satisfaction of your prospects, but you still need to wrap up your sales message. First, alert them to the importance of what you're about to say. Replace words that merely show organization of thought with powerful words that highlight the importance of your conclusion. Compare the organizational phrases in the first column with the "stand up and listen" phrases in the next:

ORGANIZATIONAL WORDS TO AVOID	WORDS THAT HIGHLIGHT INFORMATION
Finally	Let me leave you with this thought

| In conclusion | That's it, except for this one thing |
| In summary | And, this is important for you to remember |

Then, summarize your key persuasive points. These may be issues that bubbled forth in response to the questions you were asking during your presentation, or solutions to their pain that you want to bring to the forefront of their minds. Tie your persuasive points together with a story or example to anchor them in your prospects' minds.

Here are some examples of How to Say It:

And this is important for you to remember: Because you can change rates so efficiently, driving revenue by 4 percent is a conservative estimate. Maybe even more than increasing company profits, the ability to offer your customers an easier interface practically guarantees your success in this competitive market. Imagine that your Internet rates become a major profit center instead of the drain they are now. There is no other solution on the market today that offers the power and profit potential as ABC Software.

And that's all I have to say, except for this one thing: You've each brought up concerns about my company being small. You're right, it is. And when the Chicago Bulls' coach told Michael Jordan that he had to stop hogging the ball because there was no "I" in TEAM, Jordan shot back, "Yeah, but there is in WIN." I may be a small shop, but I'll help you win by ensuring your

customers see you're different from their other choices, by creating an image and brand they'll readily identify with, and by giving your sales team the tools they need to sell your unique image.

Let me leave you with this one thought: Finding excellent wine for your restaurant is not difficult. There are wonderful choices that any restaurant can offer. But you're not "any" one. Your affluent customers want to be treated special. They want to tell their friends about their experiences. Imagine them driving to your restaurant the next time talking about your irresistible food, your amazing desserts, anticipating the surprisingly unique and delicious wine selections you offer. You can play it safe, or you can create buzz and excitement and have your diners excited about new discoveries; that's what Hungarian wines will do for you. Wine innovation for sophisticated palates. As a new import to America—yet proven in Europe for over 300 years—this wine provides the excitement, edge, and energy your extraordinary offerings, and customers, deserve.

ASK FOR THE NEXT STEP

Your conclusion wraps up and makes your final case. It provides your prospects with a tidy package of persuasive facts and emotion to motivate them to want to say yes to you. But as Fleetwood Mac says, "Don't stop thinking about tomorrow!" Don't stop until you lay the groundwork for the sale or the next action.

Your close asks for the next step. It's not a manipulative way to trick them into saying yes or signing on the bottom line when they aren't ready. It's the logical outgrowth of the sales presentation you've had with your buyer.

Because you've been checking in with your prospect while you were delivering your sales presentation, asking questions about what they would like the next step to be is logical. If you omit this important closing step, you give up control and it's up to the buyer to say, "So then, will you be sending us an agreement?" Of course, that doesn't make much sense!

Based on your original goal for this sales conversation, be prepared with an agreement, and most certainly with your calendar! Be ready to move to the appropriate next step.

The question, after your conclusion, can be as simple and direct as:

- So, what are our next steps?
- What would you like the next step to be?
- How would you like to move forward?
- How would you like me to follow up this presentation?
- Is there anyone else you'd like me to talk to at this point?
- May I ask when you'll be meeting to review this?

When it's appropriate to be more specific, your questions will reflect that:

- Would you like to go ahead and schedule the beta test then?
- I took the liberty of preparing an agreement. At this point, are you ready to review it?
- To further determine if this really is the best option for you, I'm ready to review your month-end figures and present you with a comparison of our pricing. Is this an appropriate next step?

- Which of these plans seems like it best fits with your 2009 initiatives?
- With your approval, you can have——by——. Do I have that approval?
- If this sounds good to you, all I need to get moving on this for you is your approval here.
- Would you like us to put the alternate dates on a twenty-four-hour hold while you discuss whether these dates will work at the committee meeting tomorrow?

If the prospect resists moving forward, it's crucial to learn why. Understanding her resistance is the only way you can overcome her objections and clarify your solutions. The objective is to find out what areas you need to explain better, or what other situations that have not yet been disclosed to you need to be studied so that you can help her feel confident that she has everything to win by saying yes.

When you offer the next step, for example, "If this sounds good to you, all I need to get moving on this is your approval," and she says, "Thank you but we have two other vendors coming in to explain their solutions and we're not ready to move forward," or the ever-popular, "We need some time to think about it," be prepared to ask what is holding her back. This is where your preparation and your confidence can make the difference between a sale and nothing. Remember, you just participated in a customer-centric, solution-oriented sales conversation. If you persuaded her fully, and touched on everything that mattered to her, there really is no reason she can't cancel those other two appointments! Of course, she may want to see if she can leverage what she learns, but you want as much information as possible so that you can put her mind at ease now.

Questions you might ask are:

- Would you mind telling me/May I ask what disadvantages you see with this new process?
- What about this plan doesn't seem to be aligned with your initiatives?
- What would you like to see that I didn't address?
- Are there circumstances that I didn't uncover in my research or that we didn't talk about today?
- What did I leave out?
- What did I miss?

Listen to their responses. Of course, this tidbit of advice should be obvious, but it can be very difficult to hear what a customer is saying at this point (after all, you just had a great conversation—or so you thought). Listen for points of agreement. Step back and take the time to appreciate her perspective before providing answers. Understand that you missed something important during the presentation either because you were eager to move forward, and missed an implication, or you didn't make her comfortable enough to say what was really on her mind. Don't give any additional information until you understand her questions. Also, this is not a time to push, or make her feel unsafe, by saying, "If I can answer that to your satisfaction, can we move forward?"

What can you agree with without being defensive? (Review Part I for tips on How to Say It.) Answer the buyer's questions, recap, and ask for the next step again. In the end, if she insists on seeing the other vendors, or "sleeping on it" for any reason, it's important to respectfully accept her decision to wait and ask for an appropriate time to follow up with her later. Pushing will only annoy her and risk harming the relationship.

TAKE CONTROL OF THE Q & A

Because a good sales presentation is a *conversation* between you and your prospect, it's inappropriate to hold off their questions until the end. Remember your presentation goal: to close the sale or move to a next step. Recall, also, that you structured your presentation to move from introduction, to benefit-driven pitch, to conclusion and close. If you open the floor to questions *after* you conclude, you stand to lose control and you put the power of your presentation in jeopardy.

Imagine that you've delivered an outstanding presentation, but you had asked the committee to hold off on their questions, and now that you've concluded, you finally allow them to ask them. You hear: "Yes, I have a question. You say you can deliver on time, but there are ten blogs detailing your lack of ability to do just that. This blogger wrote, 'Whatever you do, run, don't walk, away from working with them if you have any expectation of seeing your delivery within six weeks of when they promise it to you. Their salespeople are friendly and appear to be trustworthy. They must get paid a lot to lie.' Any comment?"

It doesn't have to be that extreme. It could be one person on the committee with a different agenda and lots of friends, who, when you open the floor after your presentation, says, "Sounds good. Thank you. I think you've told us everything we need to know to stay with our current vendor." Had you been asking for questions throughout the presentation, you would have had the opportunity to surface this lack of interest and respond to it.

There are times when you have little control over the format of the presentation. You and your competition each receive the same directions: You have fifteen minutes for the presentation and ten minutes for follow-up questions. You're told that this format is "carved in stone."

First, nothing since the Ten Commandments has been carved in stone. Second, agree that you'll follow their format (because essentially you will). Then, plan to allow a shorter Q & A period, leaving a minute or so after the Q & A to present a "double close."

Stand apart from the crowd by telling your buyers up front, after you set the stage with your opening argument, that you'll take questions anytime throughout the presentation and that you'll save time at the end of the program, too. Don't promise them ten minutes for the Q & A section!

Present for fifteen minutes, stopping at various points to draw out their questions. At the end of fifteen minutes, announce the Q & A portion something like this:

"We have a *few* minutes left for discussion and additional questions. Who would like to make the first point?"

Or: "Questions? We have *some time* allotted for Q & A. We went through the information rather quickly so please tell me what you'd like me to clarify. Who has the first question?"

After about eight minutes, stop the Q & A. Look at the clock or the timer and say, "Ladies and gentlemen, thank you for your questions. We're just about out of time except that I ask you to remember this . . ." and then tie your final remarks directly to your opening argument so they remember how you'll solve the pain, not the point of the last questioner. Then, talk about the next step.

Say: Excellent, thank you. I appreciate the discussion, and please, consider this when you decide who will be your best partner in this project . . . When do you think you'll be ready to . . . ?

Say: Thank you for your questions. To sum up, then, you will not just save time, you will . . . What would you like the next step to be . . . ?

Say: Let me leave you with this thought . . . , I'll leave a hard copy of our agreement for you to review and I'll follow up with you tomorrow to learn of your decision.

As the presenter, you're in charge. Don't give up that power.

The driving force of a persuasive sales presentation is its focus on the customer. Your job is to say it so that you help your prospect understand he has a pain—a challenge, void, or situation he's experiencing, or will experience, because he isn't using your product—and that your solution is worth the money, time, or change it takes to alleviate or eliminate that pain.

Structure your message very much like an attorney would to win a neutral jury over to his point of view. Get their attention quickly by making your "case." Then, explain how the case can be solved. Provide supporting evidence for your point of view, wrap up by reminding them what they've heard, and ask for their decision. Take the opportunity throughout your presentation to "cross-examine" your prospects so that you are confident you are providing the evidence that matters in their decision, and will persuade them to render their decision in your favor. Present your ideas with respect, warmth, and friendship. By following this presentation structure, you make it easy for them to say yes to their overriding question, "Is this the best option for me and my company?"

7

Preparing For a
Powerful Presentation

*Regardless of how you feel inside, always try to look
like a winner. Even if you are behind, a sustained
look of control and confidence can give you a mental
edge that results in victory.*

—Arthur Ashe

The structure we looked at in Chapter 6 provides the basis for your powerful sales presentation. But walking into your meeting with a well-structured presentation isn't usually enough. You also need to deliver that structure with punch and professionalism to convince your prospect to move to the next step in the buying process with you.

This chapter helps you prepare yourself to confidently present your message. Filled with success secrets, you'll learn how to prepare for the conversation so that you exude confidence and competence whether you're presenting over lunch or to an audience of thousands. Here are the tips to help you prepare properly so you can perform at your fullest potential.

Every Sales Presentation Can Change Your Life

Nick Morgan, the author of the book *Give Your Speech, Change the World*, says that every presentation—whether you're a CEO selling change in the corporate culture, a sales manager selling to your sales team the need to boost monthly sales, or a sales professional attempting to influence a prospect to buy—has the potential to change attitudes. When you change attitudes, he says, "You just might change behavior. And if you change their behavior, you've changed the world in the only way that counts."

Prepare to say it as if you're ready to change the world. You'll blow your competition out of the water and get the respect, results, and recognition you deserve!

BE CAREFUL WHAT YOU TELL YOURSELF

Do you believe in your ability to present your message powerfully?

In coaching sessions with sales leaders, I often ask them to tell me exactly what they think about during the moments before they begin their presentation. Their responses typically begin with "I'm afraid that" and continue with these far too common fears:

- They won't like me.
- I'll forget everything I planned to say.
- I'll ramble and embarrass myself.
- I'll speak too fast, slow, or in a monotone.
- They won't laugh at my jokes.
- I won't be able to answer their questions.

To date, I've never asked that question and heard a sales-person say that he begins by thinking:

- I'm going to be great!
- This is going to be my best presentation ever!
- This is really going to be sweet.

Present yourself more confidently by thinking more confidently. Just the act of thinking negative thoughts destroys confidence.

Without doubt, your attitude is the primary determining factor of success. It makes sense, then, to prepare yourself to present from a positive frame of mind. You can do this by filling your head with past success instead of the fear you may feel approaching a presentation. See yourself presenting your ideas in a comfortable, persuasive manner and it is more likely happen. Of course, just seeing yourself doing it well doesn't guarantee success. But seeing yourself failing practically guarantees failure.

The use of positive affirmations is a proven way to counteract negative thinking. Listen to the words you use both to yourself and to others. Do you talk in negative or disparaging terms? For example, do you ever hear yourself talking about "trying to get ready for another road show," or "having to do another 'dog and pony show'"? Remember, it's garbage in, garbage stays! When you become aware of your negative thoughts, eliminate them by replacing the negativity and doubt with more positive thinking. As soon as you catch yourself thinking, "They will never buy this . . ." replace that distracting thought with, "They're going to be blown away by XYZ . . ." or "They're buying because I'm showing them this is the best option for them." Present to your goal, not to your worst fear, if you want to deliver a powerful presentation.

PRESENT PREPARED AND POISED

Steve Jobs is known for his "off the cuff" speaking style. The reality is far different. He appears to be speaking spontaneously only because he has spent hundreds of hours preparing. No different from the gymnasts and contortionists at Cirque du Soleil (okay, a little different) or anyone else who makes what they do look easy, Jobs practices and rehearses everything, and then does it again and again and again!

In an article for *BusinessWeek* called, "How to Wow 'Em Like Steve Jobs," (February 6, 2006), Carmine Gallo writes, "Jobs unveils Apple's latest products as if he were a particularly hip and plugged-in friend showing off inventions in your living room. Truth is, the sense of informality comes only after grueling hours of practice. One retail executive recalls going to a Macworld rehearsal at Jobs' behest, then waiting four hours before Jobs came off the stage to acknowledge his presence. Rude, perhaps, but the keynotes are a competitive weapon." Your sales presentations can be, too, if you're willing to prepare yourself for the conversation.

It's not enough to know what you're going to say; it's only enough when you've practiced and polished what you're going to say and are so comfortable with your presentation that you can relax and just say it.

Practice, Practice, Practice

Some charismatic salespeople have had great previous success talking "off the cuff" or "shooting from the hip." They use their intuition, inborn charm, and gut instinct to present themselves in a charismatic manner. Though it may work on occasion, speaking with little or no preparation catches up to even the most charming salesperson. Luck is not a success strategy!

Consider this: Anyone who does anything well practices. Presenting ideas in a professional, polished, persuasive manner takes as much practice as skiing, ballet dancing, and golfing (okay, maybe not as much as playing golf!). The answer to the joke, "Excuse me, mister, but how do I get to Carnegie Hall?" is "Practice, practice, and practice some more." The same holds true for sales presentations. You deliver a polished performance only when you take the time to study and apply best practices to your presentation, practice before presenting, and evaluate yourself after each one to determine what went well and what needed more fine tuning for the next time.

It's important to find a practicing method that works best for you.

I practice best at my keyboard. I type my presentation as I say it aloud. I have not found success in practicing in front of a mirror (I tend to check out the status of my hair color or latest "laugh line") and I certainly can't concentrate on my points if I envision my decision makers naked. (Who came up with that ?!)

Because I like using humor when I present, I circle anything that I plan to say that is funny (at least to me!) in red. A quick glance at my notes, during my preparation, tells me if I've evenly distributed the humor. I highlight interactive exercises and questions in green to determine if I've developed enough check-in questions throughout my presentation.

Once I have the presentation organized, I practice pieces of it. I take my notes with me wherever I go, and practice sections of the presentation at a time. I get comfortable with the opening first, then the conclusion, supporting evidence, and the questions I'll ask to move the sale forward. I pay particular attention to how I'll transition from one point to the next after I'm comfortable with my main points. No matter how often I present or how often I've practiced, I always rehearse my opening, conclusion, and close on the day of the presentation. I review with my PowerPoint slides, and review what I'll say to move from one to the next.

It doesn't matter how you choose to practice as long as you find a way that lets you feel comfortable on your presentation day so that your buyer can relax and feel the same way.

Have Notes Ready to Use

One way to prepare for a winning presentation is through the creation of notes. When you have well-prepared notes, you know that nothing can throw you off your game because all you need to get back on point is a quick glance at them. Distractions, like a decision maker's phone ringing, a server dropping a dish while you're speaking, or even an unexpected question, won't faze you. You'll be able to maintain your professionalism, poise, and polish regardless of what happens around you.

Using notes, as long as you don't simply read them to

your prospects, lets them know you value them and respect their time. The note-writing process also helps you organize your thoughts, make changes, and create a sales presentation that is customer-centric, persuasive, and powerful.

Knowing that you have good notes to refer to also eliminates the need to memorize. Taking the time to memorize your opening to get through those first few scary seconds is one thing. Attempting to memorize your entire presentation is another. Even if memorizing is comfortable for you, don't depend on it! When you count on your memory and then (inevitably) forget a word or phrase during the actual presentation, everything goes blank. That's when you start "tap-dancing" and your buyer knows it.

Your preparation goal should not be memorization, but relaxation. By eliminating the worry over forgetting your information or what you want to say next, you can put all your energy into a great delivery for the customer's sake.

As I explained, when I create a presentation, I initially type out every word. Then, as I practice, I type fewer words, and focus on key words and strategic points. With each practice, I eliminate more words. My goal is to be able to look at only one to three key words, for each main point, to jolt my memory into remembering the complete argument or story.

Sometimes I write my key points on sticky notes so that I can have a visual of the presentation flow. Using sticky notes also makes it easy to alter the order of the presentation.

Tips for creating notes:

- Use key words only. Don't write full sentences, no matter how good the statement may sound while you're creating it. Notes are helpful only when you can glance at them to know where you are and where you're going. Full sentences can't be absorbed in one glance. Also, if you use full sentences for speaking points, you'll have a greater tendency to want to read from your notes. No one wants to hear you read!

- As you rehearse, determine which key words remind you of your entire thought. If you can't reduce them to one to three words, keep working and practicing until you can.

- Write your notes in a font large enough to see! Remember, you want to be able to look quickly to find the information you need. That doesn't happen with 12-point Times New Roman font!

- Icons or other graphic representations can be used in place of words in your notes. Colors can help, too. Let's say you have three supporting points, but realize that with discussion, you may have time to address only one. Circle that point in a bright color, highlight it, or type it in a different color. That way, when you look at the clock, and your notes, you'll quickly know which point is most important. Keep colors consistent. All main points can be in black, and subpoints in blue (or whatever consistent color scheme you choose).

- Some sales presenters work from note cards, usually 3 by 5 index cards, with each card representing a unique point. If you do this, always number the cards and keep them in order with a ring binder. If you staple them, you spend too much time smoothing down the card you want to use, and if you clip them, when the clip pops off (usually in the direction of your decision maker), you can lose track of your presentation order. A snap ring, or a climber's carabiner keeps the cards together.

- Almost all presentations have time limits. To stay on target, add notes that remind you when you're a quarter of the way through, halfway, and three-quarters complete. That way, if you see that you're at your halfway mark, but you've spoken for only five minutes out of a thirty-minute presentation, you'll be aware that you should slow down, take questions, or let your audience know you'll be done a bit early! You can add notes to remind yourself to "ask for question" or other cues you're concerned you may forget.

Tips for using notes:

- Practice with your notes and with everything else you'll use during the presentation. Consider where you'll place them when you speak. Will they be on a lectern, on a table in front of you, on a desk next to you? Practice with them from that position.
- If your hand shakes and your notes are in your hand, your buyers will lose confidence in what you're saying. Place your notes on a table or desk in a place where you can see them. If there is no table, put them into a small binder or note pad that you can hold as you speak so your shaking is not visible.
- Don't play with your notes! Don't roll them up like a scroll and bang them into the palm of your other hand, on the table, or anyplace else! In fact, it's best to place your notes on something instead of in your hand. When clients and I review videotapes of their sales presentations, they are always so surprised to see what they were doing as they spoke. Avoid the temptation to play so your buyers focus on your message and not your antics.
- If you use PowerPoint slides as your notes, always bring a hardcopy backup. Don't depend on the technology

working when you need it the most. Also, remember that bulleted lists, slide after slide, are monotonous. When I use PowerPoint to stay on track, I'll place one or two key words on a slide, use a giant font, and make the words bold. Or I'll use great photos to talk to my point. Show benefits on your slides, not the home office.

- If you quote passages of information and include those on your PowerPoint slides, let your buyers read the slides. You don't need to read what they can. Make the font large enough so that they can see the words! Use the quote as a springboard to one of your own points because the quote by itself is meaningless, no matter how deep or moving.

CREATE QUESTIONS TO ASK AND ANSWER

In the previous chapter, we talked about how to handle Q & A during your presentation so you can make your most compelling argument. Before the presentation, it's important to anticipate and prepare for those questions.

Make a list of every question you think your audience could possibly ask you. Run through your presentation, point by point, to determine what questions could be generated as a result. Of course, you can't think exactly as they will, but try to become your customers. You know that they're wondering if you're the best option for them out of all available possibilities. If you were in their shoes, what would you want to know? It might make sense to want to include answers to all the questions you come up with in your presentation. Realistically, however, that isn't possible. You don't want to bore them with answers to questions they may not have, and you don't want to fill your presentation with information that may just be overkill. The point of the presentation, after all, is to persuade them that you are the best alternative because you can help them drill the best holes, not because you make the best drills, so you'll need to keep it focused. But if you take the time to list questions that could pop into their minds, and rehearse your responses, you'll enjoy added confidence as you present.

Another tip is to prepare questions that you'd like the audience to ask you. This is helpful for times when, for whatever reason, you have a particularly quiet group. For example, let's say that you're in the middle of your sales presentation to a board of directors, and you want to check in with them. Based on your research, however, you know that there is disagreement among board members regarding the best path to follow in securing the service you're pitching. The most senior people want to maintain the status quo, and the more junior people want to work with you. You know that if you ask, "So, how does that apply here?" or "What questions can I answer for you?" or "Does this sound like something that might interest you?" you're not likely to get any comments, questions, or feedback. To be certain the points are made, prepare a list of questions you'd like them to ask. Then, when you ask for questions, and there is dead silence, say, "A question I thought you might ask is" and then ask, and answer, the question. Here are some other ways to express this:

A question I'm sometimes asked at this point is . . .
I was wondering if you might like to know the answer to . . .
A question some boards have is . . .

When you're presenting to a large group, you can also prepare questions you'd like them to ask on 3 by 5 cards. This is particularly effective when you're pitching at a customer event or other meeting with twenty-five or more people. Before you begin your presentation, ask select attendees if they'd be willing to ask this question (the one written out for them on your card) when you mention that it's time for questions. Some people will be unwilling to do this, and others will be happy to help you out. Of course, you don't want to ask the CEO if she'll ask a question for you to answer! Even if the person reading the question says, "Peter asked me to read this," no one will mind. You'll just look that much more prepared.

PREP THE ROOM FOR MAXIMUM ATTENTION

There is no sense in delivering your message if no one is paying attention because the room is uncomfortable, too dark to see, or has too many distractions. As the presenter, you can almost always control these variables. The key is to arrive at the presentation venue, or your client's office, early—preferably before your customers arrive. Only then can you take control of the room environment. If you're presenting at 2 p.m., ask if you can arrive while they're at lunch so that you can scope out the room and set up.

As always, the primary concern is with your buyer's comfort, not your own. Look over the room from their perspective. If the chairs aren't arranged so that they can easily see you and your presentation materials, rearrange them! Naturally, you can't make changes to the position of a marble boardroom table, but you can move a projection screen so that everyone can see both you and it.

What other distractions might keep your audience from watching and listening to you? Here are some ideas:

- If there are windows, draw the drapes so people aren't tempted to daydream about being outside. Ideally, the room will have the type of drapes that still allow light in. If not, it's still best to close them because, no matter how riveting you may be, watching the ships come in on a sunny day will be much more so! Take a position away from any window when drapes can't be drawn.
- Position yourself away from the wall clock. You want your audience watching you, not the clock!
- Turn the lights up. Keep the room bright. Don't worry if your PowerPoint slides or demo video isn't quite as sharp as possible; everyone needs to see you sharply. You don't want to become the unseen voice-over for your slides.
- Be seen. When you're sitting in a meeting, stand up, at least at the beginning of your presentation (if you feel it's too formal to stand up the whole time), to make it easy for them to attend to what you're saying. Of course, if you're in a restaurant, this rule doesn't apply!

SET THE STAGE FOR A PROFESSIONAL FIRST IMPRESSION

Even before you've said a word, your customers are judging your professionalism and determining if they like you.

From the way you shake hands (firm, web to web), to the clothes you wear, they're deciding if you're someone they like and can trust.

Prepare your clothing so it "says" what you want it to say about you. To be most successful in selling, your clothing should convey respect for yourself and your buyers. There are so many acceptable styles today, but rarely are rumpled clothing, missing buttons, and unpolished shoes appropriate.

Before presenting, find out what the company dress code is. Call their Human Resources department, ask your contact what is appropriate, or check out their website for clues. Plan to dress similar to those you'll be pitching, or maybe one step more conservative (unless the point is creativity—and then do your thing!).

According to corporate image consultant Sandy Dumont, a "fashion look" for men diminishes power, yet a "high-fashion" look adds credibility for women. Men are seen as most credible when they wear blue suits, white shirts, and ties with red in them. (Yes, that is exactly why all politicians dress that way.) When men wear matching shirts and ties, especially in nontraditional colors, their "credibility diminishes dramatically," Dumont says. Women enhance credibility with "bold accessories" and appropriate makeup. Of course, this good advice is generalized. I just can't imagine a man or woman wearing an Armani suit to pitch to a group of ranchers, golf club superintendents, or Starbucks barristas, no matter what color! As hard as this is for me to say, politicians, and their handlers, get this right. They are, first and foremost, salespeople! Take a cue from the clothing they wear when presenting themselves to different groups.

Dress to help your buyers feel comfortable with you, and in what makes you feel good. If you look like you know what you're talking about, your customers will be more likely to let you talk about it!

Beyond your clothing "speaking" for you and creating that first impression in your buyer's mind, is personal hygiene. According to experts in the HR field, besides smelling clean and fresh, including your hair, body, and clothing, the next most important personal feature you can offer is clean and neat fingernails. Finally, don't try to talk with anything in your mouth. Gum, mints, etc., aren't acceptable.

BE READY—FOR ANYTHING

Murphy's Law says that if it can go wrong, it will. My corollary? The more important the presentation, the more likely it is that something will go wrong! This isn't worrisome when you're prepared for it.

Make a list of all the things that can wrong. Think about every distraction that could prevent you from connecting with your buyer, delivering a polished, professional presentation, and maintaining the sales conversation throughout your time together. Then, write down how you'll prepare yourself to handle each of those logistical and technical issues.

A few questions to consider are listed below. You already know the answers to some of these. (Hint: Prepare, focus on the customer, use notes.) We'll discuss answers to the other questions in this chapter and the next so that you can prevent them from happening. Still, stuff happens. Prepare for the worst and be happy when you don't need to implement Plan B!

What if I forget key points?

What if they ask me questions I can't answer?

What if I can't connect to the Internet and demonstrate my point?

What if my computer crashes?

What if the key decision maker has to leave early?

What if I run out of time, or go overtime?

What if they're bored?

What if I'm boring?

Being prepared for everything means that you do everything you can to eliminate the possibility of the situation going awry. If the worst happens anyway, it's a nonevent because you're prepared to deal with it smoothly and seamlessly. With that said, we've already discussed the answer to never forgetting a key point again: prepare useful notes. When your notes don't work and you realize twenty minutes after you intended to make the point that you didn't, you can do one of two things. Either ignore it and plan to follow up the presentation with an email explaining the point, or state the truth: "I forgot to also mention . . ." That's it. No big deal!

Being fearful that your buyers might ask questions that you'll be unable to answer can unnerve anyone. Again, you know the answer: Practice! And if it happens? Tell them what you do know, not what you don't. Apply the communication strategies to keep the sales conversation moving forward. For example:

> **PROSPECT:** So, can you tell me why Y is better than X? The last guy said X was much better and now you're saying Y is.
>
> **YOU:** I can provide a partial answer to that . . .
>
> **PROSPECT** (*irritated*): That's not what I asked you. I want to understand the differences before we make a decision.
>
> **YOU:** Yes, and I can tell you the characteristics of Y . . .
>
> **PROSPECT:** Fine. Now what about X?
>
> **YOU:** I can check with the office and text this information to you within the hour.
>
> **PROSPECT:** Well, that just isn't good enough. You should have known we'd be looking at your competition, too, and you should have been prepared to discuss this.
>
> **YOU:** You're right. The information I have about X is . . . I'll confirm that as soon as I contact the office.

Thankfully, most prospects are not as hostile as in this example!

Here are two don'ts:

- Don't apologize for not knowing the answer. Your apology won't make the answer appear and it only weakens your case.
- Don't say, "That's a great question," when it isn't. If it were a great question, most likely you would have been prepared to answer it. You'll lose credibility, and more, by being patronizing.

Don't Let Technical Glitches Slow You Down

Technical problems are the bane of every presenter. All systems can be working fine until the moment comes for you to show your streaming video demo! Take the pressure off yourself by planning and having appropriate backup, perhaps a mock-up, an interactive exercise, or handout, that enables you to make the same point (albeit without the drama). Don't waste your customer's time trying to reboot or troubleshoot. It's up to you to ignore the problem you're experiencing (remember the audience isn't experiencing a problem unless you make it so) and move to Plan B.

Be Prepared to Make a Great Presentation in Half the Time

Staying within the allotted time is difficult for many sales presenters. A watch, practice, and rehearsal should take care of that. As obvious as this sounds, it's often overlooked: time your presentation when you practice.

If you look at your watch while you present, your buyers will look at their watches, too. Take your watch off and place it in an inconspicuous spot near you, perhaps on the table next to your computer. Every time you advance a slide, check the time to stay within your time allotment.

Always ask your customers what is planned before and after you speak. If they have another meeting to attend, and you go overtime, they'll either need to cut you short, or stay and be annoyed that you didn't keep your word. Don't assume that because they have a break in their schedule after you present that you can cut into that time either. When you need to go a few minutes overtime, ask permission. You might say: "I need about three more minutes to finish. Is that okay with you?" or, "With your permission, I can complete this in less than fifteen minutes. Do I have your approval to continue on until ten fifteen?" Then, wait for someone to give you the okay, and if you don't hear it, thank the audience, finish your sentence, and leave!

CRAFT THREE POWERFUL PRESENTATIONS. It's such a sweet feeling when you know you can handle everything. So, when you've prepared fully, practiced well, arrived early, have sufficient backup in case of technical glitches, and then, just as you're ready to begin, your key decision maker says to you, "I have to catch an earlier flight than I had anticipated. I'll need to leave in about ten minutes," your heart drops. It won't have to, if you're prepared for that, too.

Prepare three presentations: one for the length of time you're supposed to have, one for about 50 percent of the time, and one that gets your point across in five minutes or less.

I was presenting at a lunch meeting and was told I'd have fifty minutes. Because the hotel also wanted to sell to these clients, they put on their best presentation performance, too; they served everything with white gloves and French service. Though I had twice confirmed with my contact that I'd have the allotted time, the slow service and sheer number of servers in the room eliminated the possibility of speaking until they exited. At that point, I had about twenty-five minutes to present. It was then that I wished I had prepared for this possibility! I do now, and recommend you do, too.

This advice is particularly important when your presentation is scheduled for late in the day, a Friday afternoon, or the afternoon prior to a holiday. Count on your time being cut short. This is also important to remember when you are one of many presenters making your pitch to a group in the same day. In the accounting world, this is called being part of a "beauty pageant"; you strut your stuff and then the next contestant comes in. You can bank on another presenter running overtime. You'll look like a hero if you can get them back on schedule and still present your points professionally.

Example:

An important prospect has invited you to present to the entire board at their upcoming meeting. The only time available in their agenda is the last slot at the end of the meeting, just before their reception and formal dinner. The incoming president won't be there because she has to get back for her eight-year-old daughter's dance recital, but everyone else is expected to be present. You have from 4:30 to 5:00 to make your pitch.

You're quite excited about the opportunity and prepare a dazzling thirty-minute presentation. You focus on their needs and have a wonderful twelve-minute video, that marketing just finished, to bring everything together for your emotional conclusion.

At 4:00, you can hear them through the door. It doesn't sound like a love fest either. At 4:10, the door flings open. It's the incoming president charging out the door. She doesn't look happy. At 4:32, your contact comes to the door and says, "William, I am so sorry. We had a major issue come up and we've just now agreed to table it until our next meeting. This probably isn't the best time for your presentation but we did agree that, because you're here, we should at least give you a few minutes. If you could wrap it up in under ten minutes, we'd really appreciate it. We have a reception to go to that starts at 4:45." As long as you prepared a shorter version of your presentation—one that can be done in about half the original time—you can move ahead confidently.

The third presentation, the under-five-minutes version, comes in handy when you know there is no value in presenting anything longer because your buyers aren't comfortable listening. There can be many reasons for this, including the ones already mentioned. No matter how short your presentation is, you can still use the structure discussed in Chapter 6.

In your own words, you might say:

"It's really late and I bet you are all exhausted. I appreciate your willingness to see me. Drummond said I could have ten minutes. I'm going to take only five. Is that okay? Right now you spend time on . . . We can save you that time because. . . . You'll also benefit by [another benefit to them]. This is so important because [quick story or example]. I'll send you an email after this meeting, and if you don't mind, I'll follow up with a quick phone call to each of you to answer your questions and see how you'd like to move ahead. Ladies and gentlemen, it's Miller time. Thank you."

When you've prepared to make your thirty-minute presentation in three minutes, you can be confident that, no matter what, you'll have the opportunity to represent yourself professionally.

Successful presentations don't happen by accident. Tom Fleming, one of the world's greatest runners, said, "Somewhere in the world someone is training when you are not. When you race him, he will win." Fleming's Boston marathon training advice is as true for presenting as it is for running. Prepare to be your best.

8

Making the Sales Presentation Come Alive

Scratch the surface in a typical boardroom and we're all just cavemen with briefcases, hungry for a wise person to tell us stories.
—Alan Kay, Hewlett-Packard

Until now, in Part III, we've talked about how to structure and prepare your sales message so that it's organized, customer-centric, persuasive, and professional. Without those qualities, the following chapter would be useless. But now you're ready to supplement what you've learned so that you can incorporate excitement, fun, and suspense to deliver a memorable presentation that comes alive for your customer. I'll show you how to involve more than just the senses of sight and hearing to create meaningful presentations that involve the listener, and prevent boredom—theirs and yours!

Professor J.R.R. Tolkien, author of *The Hobbit* and *Lord of the Rings*, may have been talking for customers everywhere when he said, "I warn you, if you bore me, I shall take my revenge." This chapter gives you the tips and tools to prevent that from happening.

Be Yourself

The most important characteristic of a persuasive presentation has already been discussed: it's all about the person listening, not the person delivering. With that said, the only way to reach them and extend influence is to be yourself.

When I first started providing sales training programs, a colleague of mine advised me to learn to speak without my NY accent. He told me, "No one will hire you sounding like that." So, I tried to sound like what I imagined a professional trainer would sound like. It was terrible! I was so busy trying not to be me that any semblance of a customer-centric presentation—even if my words were—was hopeless. Fortunately, for my workshop participants and my mortgage, I disregarded that advice fairly quickly. Be yourself!

The tools and real examples that you're about to read will show you how you can wow your buyers. After reading the examples, some of you may think, *I could never do that*. If you believe you can't apply these tips and techniques because your customers expect a more serious business presentation from you, step back and take a second look. Perhaps you're the one most comfortable and conditioned to present in serious mode. On the other hand, some of these ideas may be over-the-top for some individual sales presenters. Let who you are be your guide when dramatizing your presentation, because the most important thing you can do to build relationships and present powerfully is to be comfortable in your own skin.

Whatever your New York accent is, use it. Stay true to who you are, and within that framework, choose what works best for you to make your sales presentation come alive.

ALL BUSINESS IS SHOW BUSINESS!

Have you noticed how the presentation at a fine dining restaurant often makes the meal seem to taste better? The attention to detail—the way the salmon is perched gently on a layer of garlic mashed potatoes, placed on a bed of leafy spinach, surrounded by swirls of creamy sauce—elevates the dining experience from ordinary to extraordinary. In the same way, the drama and embellishments—the show biz—you add to your presentation transforms a good presentation into a great one.

Adding "show biz" doesn't mean adding sleight-of-hand fakery or being fancy. All you have to do is incorporate touches that make it more enjoyable for your buyers to listen and become engaged in your message. To sell, and to outsell the competition, always aim to add a memorable touch of excitement to your message.

One way to stand out from the crowd is to provide a dramatic experience as part of your presentation. Don't worry! You don't need to be a theater major to pull this off. You need only to think about how you can demonstrate what you're saying in a visual manner.

A simple way to do this is by creating interesting slides. That, of course, doesn't mean a bulleted list of points! Use great photos, and display only them—no words. When you want to position your product as saving money, display a graphic of money going down the drain. If you're talking about improving customer service, perhaps you can project an angry-looking client or a downward retail arrow.

In the documentary *An Inconvenient Truth*, Al Gore transformed a potentially boring PowerPoint sales presentation on global warning into an Oscar for best documentary, and sold us on his message.

Here's the great news: Gore used the identical persuasive presentation structure that I detailed in Chapter 6. Then, he took it beyond a basic solid structure by dramatizing each step of his presentation. Al Gore became a "showman."

When he wanted to emphasize a point, for instance, he climbed on to a scissor lift on the stage, and traveled up, up, and almost away. Only when he had been lifted past the stage-sized PowerPoint graphic, and above the curtain hanging from the stage, does he say, "You've heard of off the charts? Well, here's where we're going to be in fifty years." (Rent the DVD for full effect!) Gore discovered the key to making persuasive points: add drama to persuade your buyers to remember your message.

You don't have to hop on a scissor lift to make a point. A sales rep selling networking systems travels with a large glass bowl and boxes of long, thin spaghetti. Each morning before leaving to make sales calls, he pays hotel room service to boil the spaghetti and dump it in his bowl. Before reaching his destination, with the bowl full of squiggly pasta, he separates one strand of spaghetti and places it on top of the bowl. When he gets to his client's office, he puts the bowl in the middle of the desk or table, and begins his presentation by highlighting their pain. He points to the bowl, and says, "Based on what you've told me, this is how your network looks today. When you work with us (he lifts the single strand of spaghetti and continues), this is how it will function. Let me show you how we can do that for you."

When Ben Cohen, of Ben & Jerry's Homemade Ice Cream, had the opportunity to present his views on child welfare reform to the Senate Intelligence Committee, he was given fifteen minutes to sell his message. He could have used slides showing horrific conditions that some children in America must live in; he could have quoted statistics and laser-pointed at charts, graphs, and tables. He did none of that. Instead, he brought packages of Oreo cookies for each member of the committee. As he handed out the packages, he reportedly gave these directions: I'd like you to open the boxes and construct two towers with the cookies. One tower should be three cookies tall, and for the other, I'd like you to pile up seventeen cookies."

At first no one moved. Was it a joke? When no other information was forthcoming, some members of the committee opened their packages. With nothing else to do, they started building towers! When Ben noticed that most everyone had their two towers built, he stepped next to a newly constructed tower of seventeen cookies. Pointing at it, he said, "This is what we, in America, spend billions and billions of dollars on, for things like . . ." and he listed a bunch of well-known "pork barrel" projects like bridges to nowhere, an eight-lane highway leading to a tiny village, etc. He waited a moment for the Senators to process that information. Then, pointing to the three-cookie tower, Ben said, "This, ladies and gentlemen, is what we spend on the children of America." He paused. "I think this is wrong." And he walked out.

The drama of the demonstration, the unexpectedness of

using cookies in the Senate chambers to prove a point, the ease with which he pointed out the "pain" and made his message clear, was striking.

Here are some additional examples of show biz to create a persuasive message:

This sales manager pitches the state of Hawaii as a meeting destination to association executives, meeting planners, and boards of directors. She walks in to her presentation and prominently places two bottles of liquid, and a glass of water, on the table so that everyone in the room can see them. One bottle has been prepared with a mix of water and a cola product. On that one, she places a label with the word "Mexico." The other bottle is filled with even more cola and less water, making the water appear quite dirty. She labels that bottle "Brazil." The glass of drinking water is labeled "Hawaii." She doesn't mention or refer to the water sitting between them. As she concludes her presentation, she says, "Oh, and just one more thing." She points to the bottle labeled Mexico and says, "Water in Mexico, $2.25. [*Pause.*] Water in Brazil, $4.30. [*Pause.*] Water in Hawaii?" She takes a sip from the glass, swallows, and says, "Priceless."

Imagine that you're the salesperson following that dramatic demonstration and you represent the country of Mexico. Because competitors are usually asked to wait outside while their competition presents, you have no idea how striking her visual demonstration was.

You, however, are prepared to make your ideas come alive. Because you also did your research prior to arriving, you knew the board was considering Hawaii, too. So, you've filled two money bags from a local bank with surprises. One bag, you've stuffed with U.S. dollars and some sand. In the other bag, you've placed a few pesos, two margarita glasses, and a small bottle of Tequila. When it's your turn to present, you move her water out of the way so they're no longer looking at it, and place your bags there. When you're ready to close, you take the first bag and let the contents spill out. Next, you pick up the "Mexico" bag, set up the margarita glasses, and spill out the few coins. You say, "Oh, and one more thing to remember. We're half the price of other choices and twice the fun!" You can further embellish this presentation with Mexican music playing in the background, and tacos, chips, and salsa that you pass around, in a bowl that says, "Mexico—Half the price and twice the fun," painted on the sides. When you leave, remember to leave the bowl of chips. They'll be eating your chips—and remembering you—throughout the next presenter's program.

By adding drama—show biz—that is appropriate for your buyers, you create a memorable experience and a winning presentation.

GET THEM INVOLVED

Another way to boost the significance of your presentation is to have your audience become a part of it.

The most basic way of involving them, of course, is by asking questions. This simple change elevates your presentation from a monologue to a dialogue—a true sales conversation—and gives you the opportunity to clarify expectations and overcome objections. We've talked about checking in with them and preparing questions in earlier chapters.

Aside from the more traditional Q & A format that most salespeople rely on, you can also choose to get creative.

A giant leap in the intensity of engagement occurs when you motivate your prospects to talk about *your* product's benefits and features during your pitch. Depending on how open your decision makers are, you can do this with the promise of prizes, or just your enthusiastic expectation.

Here's an example: I was the featured guest speaker at a lunch meeting being sponsored by the Renaissance St. Louis Grand & Suites Hotel. As the sponsor of this association meeting, their director of sales was given ten minutes to speak about the hotel.

The day before this, I had attended a different state's chapter meeting. That sponsor also had ten minutes to pitch her product in return for underwriting the price of our meals. She was nothing less than awful. The best one could say is that she was prepared, but poorly. She must have had 115 slides to show in her ten minutes and intended to give us more factual information about her company than anyone would ever need or want to know. Her prospective customers tuned her out after just a few minutes of her information overload. She not only didn't deliver a persuasive presentation; she may have harmed her reputation by giving such little thought to who her buyers were and what they needed to know.

Sitting in St. Louis, I was expecting a similar data dump, and as the next speaker, I was thinking about what I could do to further dramatize my opening to wake them up from a boring start. I needn't have worried! The DOS began, not by welcoming us, or thanking us, but with an involving question that addressed the elephant in the room. In this case, the elephant—the thing that was obvious to everyone— wasn't a negative issue; it was that everyone in the room already knew all about the hotel. It had been there about

ninety years, and there was little he could say that would
be new or exciting. He asked, "How many of you know
something about this hotel?" He waited for a response.
When he saw hands go up, he continued. "Excellent," he
said, "I'll give you about three minutes so that each table
can come up with a factoid about your experience with the
Renaissance St. Louis Grand. Everyone that can tell us
something will win a prize for their table." The room
started to buzz.

Three minutes later, he interrupted our discussions
about his hotel. "Okay. Which group would like to go first?
The best prize goes to the first group to answer." Hands
shot into the air. It sounded like a first grade class, "Me,
me, me, pick me here, over here!"

When he pointed to a woman at the fourth table, her entire table cheered. She said, "The St. Louis Grand started as
the Statler Hilton in 1924."

"Congratulations, you're right! The hotel started as a
Statler in 1917 [*notice how he corrected the year*] and Hilton
joined the family in 1928 [*finished the correction*]." He handed
each person at the table a bottle of hand lotion with the hotel's name on it. Was it a critical selling point? Probably not.
But his customers were engaged, enjoying an emotional
connection with his product. After all, the goal of his presentation wasn't to sell rooms at that moment, but to recon-
nect his buyers with the product.

"Which table wants to be next?" Again, hands flew into
the air. The next table received hotel soaps after one
woman told about her mother and father getting married
in the ballroom we were in. She commented how great the
renovation job was because it perfectly recaptured the ele-
gance of the fifties with all the richness of today! When

everyone in the room looked around, now seeing the room through her eyes, I could see heads shaking in agreement, and watched as his customers became more and more animated as they waited to tell about their experiences with the hotel. Eventually, every table got involved, and everyone received a take-home gift (advertising the hotel). He concluded by summarizing a few of the more emotional comments they had made, and closed by saying, "So for those of you who'd like to see how we've remodeled the other areas of the hotel, after lunch, I'd be honored to take you on a tour. Let's eat!"

Seeing the beauty in this interactive presentation isn't hard. His customers (meeting planners who could book rooms in his hotel) provided testimonials about the hotel. If he had said the same things, it would have been perceived as just another data dump. If he had said, "The hotel is great for you because . . ." there would have been a collective silent groan! When his customers spoke for him, however, they added to the existing social proof that his hotel was indeed great. His presentation was forceful because he engaged them by involving them.

Here is an example of a quieter type of involvement: A financial advisor places a bag on the desk between himself and his clients. It's filled with pennies. As he pushes the bag over to his clients' side of the desk, he directs them to stack the pennies according to how much they'd like for their retirement. He begins his consultative approach by suggesting they think first of how much they'd like to leave their children. Each penny, he tells them, equals $1,000. As they build, he continues to show them how he can help them achieve their goals. Startling? Maybe not. Dramatic effect to keep buyers engaged? Absolutely!

Duke Ellington said, "You've got to find some way of saying it without saying it." Think beyond lists and words to
demonstrate your message more dramatically.

ADD HUMOR

There are still some people today who believe that the ideal
presentation is dull, serious, and "all business." Laughter is
good for the soul. It creates connection among people, enhances likability, and may even increase productivity. It
also makes presentations more fun, lively, and memorable.

What's wrong, however, is the all-too-frequent "start
with a joke" sales presentation routine. You can start with a
humorous true story, but please, not a joke. When you want
to use humor, first consider if you're funny! If you're not,
plan the humor by inserting humorous real-life stories into
your initial script. (Review the section on using persuasive
humor in Chapter 2.)

When you do tell an entertaining story, don't laugh at it
until your audience does. It's a pretty foolish feeling being
the only one laughing! Tell the story and wait for them to
get it. If no one laughs, keep going as if you, too, intended it
as a serious anecdote.

If you just can't help yourself and laugh aloud—and
you're the only one laughing—say something like, "Well, I
thought that was funny!" If they like you, or feel sorry for
you, they'll probably laugh to put you at ease. The problem
is you won't know if they're laughing at you—or your story.

PRESENTING TO "FRIENDS"

Wow them from the first impression to the last.

It's clear that there is more than one more way to make a presentation come alive. This last tip isn't about the presentation itself, yet it's an amazingly simple way to create a sense of wow and make your presentation memorable: Be a host.

As we discussed in Chapter 7, you want to arrive at your presentation early enough so that you can get a feel for the room and orchestrate it so that it's easy and comfortable for your buyers to listen to you. There are two even more important reasons to get there early: You can control their first impression of you, and you can make "friends." If the first time they see you, you're rushing in, perspiring, not paying attention to them, and hurriedly setting up your computer, you've lost the opportunity to make a professional first impression and meet them more as a partner than a vendor.

When you're making a formal sales presentation to multiple decision makers, plan to be there early enough to mingle with them over coffee, over lunch (when possible), or while they're all talking informally before they sit down to get into their analytical "okay, let's hear what you have to say" mode. When you do this, you almost become one of them. You have the chance to ask questions, confirm details, and joke around on an informal basis, and when you begin your sales presentation, they look at you differently and you feel more comfortable with them. You've "broken bread" together. When you're presenting to a group, I always recommend that you arrive at least one hour before the sales meeting, and earlier if, for instance, you know there is a planned break at 9:45 a.m. and you start at 11:30 a.m. You can always practice your presentation, do computer work, or make phone calls while you wait for your turn to present.

Because last impressions are as important as the first ones you make, when you've concluded and closed your presentation, continue acting as their host. Even though you're likely on their turf, do everything you can to make them feel comfortable asking questions that they may not have wanted to ask in front of the others. Leave your equipment alone and don't clean up after yourself. Let them see you. Remember that your presentation isn't over until you are no longer in the presence of your customer. Become a host and a friend.

Fast Company magazine wrote, "Unoriginality is a sin." When you sound like everyone else, your customers must rely on price to help them with their buying decision. Don't sound like your competition. Spice up your presentation! Be comfortable presenting your message with a bit of show biz.

Dramatic flair, in a manner that suits your personality, helps your customers grasp your message and keeps it fresh in their minds. It doesn't matter if you're presenting your message business-to-business, to individual consumers, or you're selling to one or one thousand, when you make the sales conversation come alive, you honor your listener and yourself. As Ed Sullivan used to say, make it a *"rrrrreally big shew!"*

PART IV
Selling It in Writing

The ability to sell in writing is fast becoming a survival skill.
—Sales and Marketing *magazine*

Like every other form of communication we've discussed, email and other written messages can help us start and maintain the sales conversation. When written in a clear, concise, direct, positive, and customer-centric manner, they persuasively communicate our sales messages. When poorly written, they ruin reputations, cause confusion, and lose sales.

According to the Pew Study, writing email is the most common function of Internet usage. In fact, globally, we're writing so many of them that breaking through the clutter, and getting the results, respect, and recognition we deserve, is becoming more of a challenge each day.

In Part IV, we'll focus on email as a selling tool. I'll detail a writing process that will save you up to 80 percent of the time you now spend writing. You'll also learn how to write more efficient and more effective messages, how to change your style to get your message read, and what you must know about email to be safe, smart, and savvy.

Email is today's "killer app." You have just a few seconds to grab your prospect's attention, and the stronger your writing, the more likely you are to make the connection that can result in profitable sales. Good writing skills give your customers confidence, too. Though your skill at writing doesn't actually change the quality of your products or the effectiveness of your solution, it does convey attention to detail. That's important to every buyer. Additionally, when you promise excellence, and your writing isn't, suspicion is cast on the validity of your claim. Knowing this, it's, as *Sales and Marketing* magazine said, a matter of *survival* to write in a respectful, customer-focused manner so your message will sell.

9

The Secret to Persuasive Sales Writing

Good writing is essential for almost any career,
and with today's advanced technology, the need to write
well has never been more important.
—Bob Costas

A common thread among successful people is the ability to write persuasively. In the selling profession, this skill is almost a secret weapon, one that practically guarantees the ideas you propose will be well considered. The challenge is that, over the years, many salespeople have depended more on their charismatic personalities than on their ability to persuade and influence with the written word. That no longer works today.

Email is the communication choice for most business interactions in the global marketplace, and excellent writing skills are critical. In fact, as research has recently proven, buyers make split-second decisions about you based purely on the way you write. (This really shouldn't come as a surprise; we judge others by all sorts of criteria that may have nothing to do with who they really are!) Without good writing skills, you have one less tool in your box to make your point, build and cement relationships, and create a positive impression.

In this chapter, we'll detail the skills necessary for writing a customer-centric and persuasive message so that you can use email to build relationships and set yourself apart from the competition. We'll begin with the three-step writing process that can save you up to 80 percent of the time you currently spend writing. This prewriting process includes planning, doing, and checking.

STEP 1. PLAN YOUR MESSAGE

Writing a letter that sells your message starts with knowing your purpose. By taking the time to prepare your message goal, you can easily accomplish it. Writing without a clear purpose is pointless—and it wastes good selling time, too!

Wherever I'm speaking in the world, when I make that claim, I can see most heads nod in agreement. There is always one sales professional in the group, however, who shouts out, "Oh, I know *my* purpose. It's to close the sale!" Maybe you were thinking that, too.

The challenge with "close the sale" thinking is that it is too broad to serve you well. By considering exactly what you want from the *specific* email or proposal you're sending and crafting it accordingly, you're more likely to persuade your buyer to listen to your message.

USE PLANNING QUESTIONS TO DETERMINE YOUR PURPOSE. The first step in the three-step writing process is an analytical step and requires that you take two minutes (or less) to answer four planning questions prior to beginning your sales message. The two minutes you take on the front end greatly simplify the task of writing. The planning questions are:

- Why am I writing?
- What do I want to say?
- What do I want to accomplish?
- What is the next step? Is it clear to the reader?

The first two answers should concentrate entirely on the recipients of your message; they should reflect their needs and their success, not yours. Until you're comfortable with this process, you may want to look at these questions in this way:

- Why should they want to read what I've written?
- What can I say that will matter to them?

The third question is about you. The answer is your driving reason for writing in the first place. The last question requires a clearly stated action that your buyer, or you, will take next, plus a motivating reason for taking that next step.

The actual words used to answer the planning questions can be helpful in the writing of the email, but they are not necessarily used. When thinking through your purpose, then, don't be concerned with any word choices. Your only goal is to analyze your message's intended outcome.

We'll review the answers to these questions with each example in this chapter. It will be helpful for you to write your answers to the questions for each example before you look at mine. When our answers don't align, it may only mean that you and I had different writing goals. That's fine! The important point is to have a writing goal.

Example:

Your client, Jessica, had asked you to hold space for her mother's May 16 retirement celebration. You sent an agreement to her and have not received it back. At this point, you don't know if she is still planning to hold the party in your hotel. You'd like an update on the decision because you cannot hold the room past tomorrow at 5 p.m.

When writing to follow up with her, the overarching goal is to communicate in a manner that sets you apart by showing your customer you care about her success. Here, then, are my answers to the planning questions:

- Why am I writing? (Or: Why should she want to read what I've written?) Because her mother will have a wonderful party here.
- What do I want to say? (Or: What can I say that will matter to her?) Your mother's party will be impressive in the Leash Room.
- What do I want to accomplish in this email? Persuade her to sign the agreement I attached to confirm the space for the party.
- What is the next step? Is it clear to the reader? To confirm the space for the party, she needs to fax the agreement back before the end of the workday tomorrow.

It's easy to see that thinking through the true writing goal, rather than impulsively writing simply because-I-don't-see-the-agreement-from-her-yet, allows you to craft a message that sells for you.

STEP 2. WRITE IT!

The first step to writing persuasively is planning. The next step in the process is doing it. With your outcome clearly in mind, draft your message. Create. Get your thoughts and words on the screen. The "do" phase is a creative step and requires only that you keep moving forward—talking your words onto the screen—no matter what. If your punctuation is poor, ignore it at this point. If your sentences ramble or you can't think of the exact word you want, don't be concerned. We'll get to that in the third step of the writing process. For now, use only the creative portion of your brain without any critical analysis.

The first draft of your email to Jessica might look like this:

Hi Jessica,

Your mother will be so excited when she sees how impressive the Leash Room looks for her retirement party. She'll be proud to invite her family and colleagues to such a prestigious location and take away memories that she'll always remember.

To confirm the beautiful Leash Room for the party, please sign and fax the attached agreement to me at 555-555-5555. As long as I receive it by 5 p.m. tomorrow, I can still guarantee the space for you.

I'm looking forward to meeting your mother and working on the details with you.

Best,

Matthew Adam

STEP 3. CHECK YOUR WRITING

The third step in the writing process is to check your work. It's your time to proof, edit, and polish. Now is the time to swap neutral, boring or incorrect words for more powerful ones, spell-check, and correct.

In reviewing the message to Jessica, I notice that my last sentence talks about what *I* want. No different from any other type of sales conversation, in writing you want the last words to reflect value to the customer. I also need to improve some of my word choices to make my message more vivid and maintain a positive focus on my reader. Here is my revision, using all three steps:

Hi Jessica,

Your mother will be delighted when she walks into the elegant Leash Room for her retirement party. She'll be proud to have her family and colleagues around her as she celebrates this momentous occasion.

To confirm the beautiful Leash Room for the party, a signed agreement is necessary. By faxing back the attached agreement to me before 5 p.m. tomorrow, I can guarantee the room for you. After that time, we'll need to recheck availability.

As soon as I receive the agreement, I'll phone you to talk about the details so that we can help you create an event your mother will remember always.

Best,

Matthew Adam

Keep in mind, of course, that your word choices may be more subdued or more enthusiastic than mine. Let *your* personality shine!

Here is another example.

Imagine this: You have just taken over the territory from Michelle, who was promoted and is now working out of the Boca Raton office. You decide the best way to introduce yourself is to send an email to your new clients.

Without thinking through the message purpose, many salespeople would mistakenly assume that they needed to write to introduce themselves. That would result in an email something like this example:

Hi Ann,

My name is Deborah and I'm writing to introduce myself to you. I'm your new account manager and I've taken over for Michelle, who is now located in our Boca office. My background includes three years working with this company in the Southwest before transferring here. Additionally, before joining this company, I worked on cruise ships, so you can see I'm a real people person.

I'll be in touch with you within the next few weeks. In the interim, if you have questions, please feel free to call me at 555-555-5555.

All the best—
Deborah Jackson

By taking the time to plan the message, the writer can be much more persuasive; she can sell, not just tell. Let's look at the planning questions to see what Deborah could have included to make her email more effective:

- Why am I writing? To let my customer know she'll still receive the same great service as she did when working with Michelle.

- What do I want to say? Her account will be serviced seamlessly.
- What do I want to accomplish in this email? I want her to recognize who I am and take my call when I phone; I also want to keep her business through the account rep switch.
- What is the next step? Is the action clear? I'll follow up with her to make her life as easy as possible.

Here is how the draft of Deborah's sales message might look after planning her customer-centric purpose:

Hi Ann,

I'm writing to let you know that you will continue to receive the same great service as always. Even though Michelle is moving to our Boca Raton office, your account will be serviced seamlessly. I'll phone you in a few weeks to review your needs.
All the best,
Deborah Jackson

Now that the message is created, you can go back to upgrade it! Sam Horn, author of *POP!*, says, "Draft, then craft!" John Steinbeck suggested the same when he advised writers to, "Never correct until the whole thing is down. Rewriting in process is usually found to be an excuse for not going on."

In revising the draft, here are some questions to ask yourself:

- Does the opening sentence matter to my client? Can I make it even more compelling from her perspective?

- Do I present my information in the most positive way possible, emphasizing what can be done rather than what can't be?
- Do I choose words that resonate for my buyer, or am I using company jargon?
- Is my action step as specific as possible? Will the buyer wonder what that next step is or who is responsible for taking it?
- Have I been clear in what I want? Have I asked for a signed agreement rather than an "update"?
- Have I been thorough yet concise?
- Have I eliminated information that isn't important to my buyer?
- Have I provided an important reason for my buyer to do what I'm asking?

Here is a much more persuasive revised draft:

Hi Ann,

Michelle Glick asked me to write to you. She wanted to ensure that you continue to receive excellent service as she transitions to her new position in Boca Raton. Please know that you will continue to get the best prices and our very best values. I'll phone you June 16 to introduce myself more officially, and to talk with you about a technology that is just being released that may further simplify your distribution process.
Wishing you all the best,
Deborah Jackson

This last version is direct, clear, concise, and to the point. It's original because it doesn't sound like the typical introductory letter that focuses on the writer. The purpose is clear: help the buyer feel comfortable with her new sales manager.

GIVE YOUR BUYER A REASON
TO RESPOND TO YOU

A discussion of the four planning questions wouldn't be complete without extra emphasis and explanation of the last question: Is the next step clear? This question, as mentioned, is intended to prompt you to think about who will need to act to move to the next step. A secondary question to ask yourself is: Why will the customer want to take/receive this action? What's in it for him if he takes my call, calls me back, buys this product, signs the agreement?

You can help him give you the result you want by taking control of the next step rather than expecting him to follow up with you. You'll see the similarity between writing and presenting when I say that you don't want to force the reader to bear the burden of following up with you. Whenever possible, take control of the next step. Of course, if you're sending thousands of sales letters, it will be difficult to follow up on each one, but then, I'd rethink that strategy anyway. How customer-centric can one be in a situation like that?

Follow the action statement with a persuasive reason why the buyer should want to take it, or have it happen. People like to have a reason for what they do. While explaining research conducted by Harvard social psychologist Ellen Langer, Robert Cialdini, in his book *Influence: The Psychology of Persuasion*, found that you can increase compliance by about 30 percent just by providing a reason for a request. Max Sackheim said, "Whenever you make a claim or special offer . . . come up with an honest reason why, and then state it sincerely. You'll sell many more products this way." He should know! A professional copywriter, he wrote an ad that successfully ran for forty years and he originated the idea of the book-a-month club!

Boost persuasiveness by providing a reason that matters to the customer with a specific follow-up date.

Here are a few examples of effective closings. You'll find a striking similarity between these and previous samples you've seen throughout this book since, naturally, the building blocks to successful sales communication will always be linked, no matter how you're connecting with your prospect:

INSTEAD OF: Thank you for your consideration. (*This is polite but not persuasive.*)
SAY: I'll call you Monday morning to talk about how your guests can enjoy a vacation they'll always remember!

INSTEAD OF: If these details are something you'd like to consider, it would be my pleasure to send you additional information.
SAY: I'll phone you tomorrow to see if this meets with your approval. We can then talk about the shipment options available to your international offices.

Provide All the Details They Need

When you must ask your buyers to follow up with you, and sometimes that is the reality of sales, give them all the information they need to find you. Provide your office number immediately following your request to call, and your fax number when you ask them to fax. It may be more convenient for you to include the pertinent information in your signature line, but make it convenient for them to see it where they need it.

> **INSTEAD OF: I'll look forward to your call.**
> **SAY: It's easiest to reach me on my direct line, 555-555-5555. As soon as I hear from you, I'll reserve the space and get to work on the meeting details for you.**

> **INSTEAD OF: Please fax this back at your earliest convenience.**
> **SAY: Please fax the agreement to 555-555-5554. As soon as I receive it, I'll confirm the details for you.**

MAKE SURE YOUR MESSAGE IS CLEAR TO *THEM*

As we've seen over and over, the core of every persuasive conversation is an unstinting focus on the buyer. This becomes especially vital in email because at the exact moment that the message moves away from the reader, the reader clicks, and you're yesterday's news! With no need to be polite, he can just delete your message.

To be persuasive, you must keep your ego in check. According to the authors Sproul and Keisler in their book, *Connections: New Ways of Working in the Networked Organization*, readers misunderstand us ten times more frequently in email than in any other form of communication. Justin Kruger, researcher and professor at the NYU Stern School of Business, showed that almost 50 percent of us overestimate our ability to communicate clearly in email. That wasn't the startling part, but this was: The reason for the misunderstanding was pure ego! We think we've said what we meant, but because we think about the message from our perspective, half the time we miss the mark.

Write so that you won't be misunderstood by constantly asking yourself: Why am I telling this to my reader? So what? How does this impact her? Why should he care?

GIVE GOOD NEWS BEFORE BAD

Once again, like all profitable sales conversations, it's smart to emphasize possibility instead of the opposite. In writing, presenting negative messages in the most positive manner possible, and presenting the good news before the bad news, is nonnegotiable. Just as someone can quickly delete an ego-centric message, he can trash your message upon reading the "bad news"—without ever seeing the positives or possible alternatives.

Points to emphasize:

TELL THE CUSTOMER . . .	DON'T TELL THE CUSTOMER . . .
How to	How not to
What is possible	What isn't possible
What criteria need to be met	What criteria weren't met
What you can do	What you can't do

Examples:

INSTEAD OF: There is no way we can deliver the package on Wednesday.
SAY: The package will be there by Thursday.

INSTEAD OF: I'm not available anytime Tuesday.
SAY: I'm available all day Wednesday, and Monday afternoon, between 1 and 5 p.m. (EST).

INSTEAD OF: A 20% discount isn't possible on this small order.
SAY: We can extend a 20% discount on orders over $1,200.

Here are full examples:

Example:
A buyer you met with last week called you on your cell phone while you were commuting to work. She apologized for phoning so early, but she was on her way to London, and needed to know if you could complete an order for her within three days. Because you were on a sales blitz all last week, you have no idea how the calendar looks or whether you can do it for her in such a short window of time. You tell her that you'll check when you get to a computer. When you get to work, you see that there is no way that you can get it for her in less than four days at your regular rate. Email her to let her know.

- Why are you writing? To tell her what you can do for her.
- What do you want to say? Here are the alternatives to make it happen.

- What do you want to accomplish? Build or maintain the relationship.
- What action as next step? As soon as she emails you with her preference, you'll take care of the details.

Hi Sharona,

As promised, I reviewed the schedule to see how we can complete the order for you within three days. We can have the job ready for you within your time frame if we print in two runs, and begin by 4 p.m. EST today. There is a surcharge of $X,XXX for the second run. Alternately, we can have everything press ready by the third day, and have your order completed in one run at close of business of the fourth day, without any additional costs. We'd also need to begin this order by 4 p.m. today.

Please let me know how you'd like to proceed and I'll take care of all the details for you.

Example:
Your company sells parasite preventative pills to veterinarians. They've improved the formulation and made the pills chewy. Previously, the pet owner had to create a way for the pet to swallow the pill. The challenge is that they cost more than the original ones. Your company plans to eliminate production of the original pills by year's end. You need to send an email to the doctors letting them know about the price increase. Find the most persuasive, customer-centric approach through planning:

- Why? To let them know that they can now offer a superior product to their pet owners.

- What? Dogs and their owners will be happier and more compliant because the pills are easier to administer; dogs will be healthier as a result; you'll be a better health care provider.
- Accomplish? Motivate them to continue to prescribe PPPs; limit resistance during office visits next month.
- Action? No immediate action.

Dear Dr. Schwartz,

Offering your patients and their parents the highest-quality medicine available is what you do each day. We've just discovered a way to make that easier for you.

As you know, PPPs are not given on a consistent basis because of the degree of difficulty administering them. The new chewy, steak-flavored PPP guarantees that every dog will beg for his monthly dosage! You'll know that your patients will never experience the pain of parasites again.

The collateral I'll leave with you when I see you next month will help your patients' families understand the need for the increase in price. It also highlights the incredible new benefits, and explains how they can keep their pet happy and healthy.

Regards,

William Brady

The more positive your presentation—whether you're face-to-face, over the phone, or using email—the easier it is to persuade them to accept your message.

To write powerful and persuasive sales messages, start with your purpose and your buyer's needs. Your customers are busy people and they need cues and clues to determine if they like you, if you're credible, and if you're interested in their success. They'll make instantaneous decisions about you and the solutions you offer based on how you compose your email message to them. When the products you and your competition provide are equal, the person who can express him or herself most clearly will make the sale. Use the four planning questions to think through why you're really writing and what you—and they—need to achieve. Do what you can to help them grasp your message and give you the result you desire.

10

Getting Your Email to Sell for You

*It's as hard to unsend a bad email as
it is to unspread butter.*
—Sue Hershkowitz-Coore

Email is used by just about everyone. But that doesn't mean it's used well. Even when an email is written in a customer-centric manner, your buyer can still reject your message. If you don't take the time to show that you care about the details and that you respect his or her time, your email is more likely to harm your sales effort than help it.

Using the planning questions and applying the three-step writing process discussed in Chapter 9 are the first steps to composing persuasive, customer-centric email. But crafting a message that breaks through the clutter and grabs your prospect's attention is the key to success.

This chapter will help you zero in on the email details that are so often overlooked. These are the finishing touches that will get your message opened, read, and acted upon.

SUBJECT LINES THAT SELL

Readers use two criteria to help them determine whether to open an email message: the author of the message and the subject line. So, when you're writing to a new prospect who won't recognize your email address, your subject line must do all the work. Surprisingly, though, many salespeople give little thought to the importance of this tool as a way to presell the message.

A good subject line helps your reader make the shift from whatever she was thinking about, to the content of your message—before she even opens it.

These tips will help your subject line convey meaning and get attention:

- Keep it short; 5–10 words are best. With that said, also make it as informative, customer-centric and thorough as possible to presell prospects on the message content.
- Design your subject line to be a summary of your message. The clearer your subject line, the easier you make it for your customer to follow through on your message.

A subject line from a sales rep to a prospect that simply says "Lunch" may seem clever at first glance. Now picture the prospect receiving this email at about 2:15 p.m., in the middle of a busy day. He glances at the subject line, looks at his watch, and deletes the message. A better choice would provide more details such as:

- Lunch meeting to discuss premium chocolates—May 15
- You're invited—Lunch meeting May 15—Premium chocolates discussion

A subject line that says, "Conference call" is just as unhelpful. Again, envision your buyer. She juggles conference calls throughout the day—every day. The subject line doesn't offer enough information or clarity. Again, a better choice would provide the details the buyer needs to participate in the call:

- Conf Call Sept 9, 11:30 a.m. (EST) Re: Jan sales meeting.

Here are some additional examples:

AVOID	WRITE
Kapalua meeting	Kapalua meeting Agenda Deadline: Dec 19
Urgent Question	Bahamas project question—Planning meeting 2/14
Please read this	Delivery Options for Invoice #2314
????	Ground Transport Question—Your advice please
Here is the report	First Draft: Sleeping Dogs Sleep

Limit punctuation in your subject line to lessen the likelihood that it will be caught by a spam filter. Today's sophisticated filters count the number of possible infractions in a message. Colors, particularly red, multiple exclamation points after a word (!!!), setting font in bold, and the overuse of punctuation in a subject line are just some of the "spam characteristics" spam programs search for. You can space the words in your subject line to make it look more appealing to the eye and easier for your reader

to read, but limit punctuation to a very few common marks. Be certain your message reaches your buyer!

Deadlines should always be included in your subject line both to encourage your prospect to open your message in a timely manner and also to help him manage his time.

INSTEAD OF: Final Day for Sale Prices
SAY: January 13: Final Day for Sale Prices

INSTEAD OF: Spec deadline
SAY: Deadline Dec 28: Specs required

You can boost the appeal of informative subject lines, too. According to Internet marketing expert Karen Gedney, a Top 10 list format is "always a winner." She believes the reason for the format's success is that not only is it catchy, but it lets the buyer know that he'll only have a list—not a data-filled pitch—to look at. Using this idea, your subject line might say:

- If you sell diet products: Top 10 reasons to start your diet now
- If you want to draw people to your family restaurant: Top 3 concerns of eating out with children
- If you sell financial services: Top 7 strategies to be ready for your child's college tuition

These interesting subject lines are great to use when you're sending a prospecting email message.

Another idea to get someone to open your email is to provide compelling research in abridged form in the subject line. Because this type of subject promises valuable content, many prospects give it the benefit of the doubt and open it. Here are some examples:

- 50% of emails insult readers. Beat the odds.
- 25% of fitness regimens add fat. Learn which ones.
- 90% of workers have back pains. Sit at your computer correctly.

The word "free," though attractive, is a surefire way to be filtered into a spam folder. Use these powerful options, instead, to get past those filters and persuade a reader who doesn't know you to open your message:

- Our treat—Lilac-scented candles with your purchase
- Lilac candles reserved for you with your purchase

Never Recall an Email

Sometimes, because we're rushing, or the phone rings and interrupts us, or *we aren't thinking*, we click Send before our message is finished. Sometimes the message is incomplete. Sometimes it has information in it that's wrong (like last year's prices).

Don't panic! Your career isn't ruined. Do not, however, attempt to recall the message! Doing so only serves to bring attention to your mistake. Depending on the mail software your client uses, you may not be able to call back the incomplete or incorrect email; she simply receives two from you—the original and the recall request. Instead, send an email with the subject line of either "Corrected message" or "Updated information":

- Corrected Message: Pl disregard [subject line of previous message]
- Update: Pl disregard [subject line of previous message]

This is not only more professional, it also reduces the possibility that your buyer will open and read your other message.

GREETINGS

Once you've gotten past the first hurdle, persuading a stranger to open your email, the next challenge is greeting him in a manner that is professional. On the surface, this doesn't seem like it should be a major issue. The dilemma is that, unlike traditional mail with its conventional salutation of "Dear [Name]," no email standard or protocol exists.

NAMES. When you and your buyer have an existing relationship, take a cue from your other communications with her. A good rule of thumb when writing to people you don't know is to use the same level of formality that you would when addressing them in person or on the phone. If you typically call them Mr. MacMahill or Ms. Goldberg, do the same when addressing them in email. If you're more informal, call them by their first name.

When writing internationally, err on the side of being too formal when you aren't sure of the proper greeting. Many other cultures are far more formal than in the United States, and you would surely lose a sale in some countries if you opted to call your buyer by his first name.

Take the time to check the spelling of your prospect's name. Always.

SALUTATIONS. When writing an email, your salutation will often depend on the formality of your industry and your relationship with the recipient. The following list consists of acceptable options for just about any industry. Take special notice of the punctuation that follows each example. When using the first name, you can opt for a comma or a dash. If you use the formal "Dear" with the last name, use a colon.

- Hi, Peyton,
- Hello, Paige,
- Good morning, Valerie,
- Good morning, Mr. Russell,
- Mary Jo—
- Dear Mr. Bodane:

Here are two salutations to avoid:

- "Greetings, Patrick." Baby boomers still remember when draft notices began with "Greetings." It's not a warm fuzzy opener for that generation.
- "Hey, Bethany."

Just as an appropriately strong (but not too strong!) handshake sets the tone for a good introduction, an appropriate salutation sets the tone in your email and encourages your prospect to continue reading. Be friendly not familiar.

SAY IT CLEARLY AND CONCISELY

The Owens Graduate School of Business at Vanderbilt University conducted a series of experiments to learn how corporate employees use email. Based on the way people wrote, they divided email users into three hierarchal groups: low, middle, and high statuses.

A combination of email etiquette and good writing determined how these writers were perceived. They found that those identified as "low status" writers:

- Use happy faces (emoticons).
- Use too many words.
- Use fluffy words.
- Often include a "motivational thought" in a signature line.
- Overuse exclamation points.

"Mid-level status" writers:

- Use email to impress rather than express.
- Write long, involved messages.
- Use jargon.
- Use email to debate points.
- Hide behind the anonymity of email.

"High status" writers:

- Write in a concise manner.
- Use short sentences.
- Write in a direct way.
- Present messages in a positive, clear manner.

Give your buyers the best first—and last—impression by positioning yourself as a concise, clear, and direct high status writer in every message you send.

CLOSE WITH CARE

Just as it's a struggle to strike the perfect tone when opening an email, the closing poses special challenges, too. What's the best closing to use? Again, your personality, your client's, and your company culture determine what is right for you. Here are some appropriate choices to consider:

- Wishing you the best—
- All the best—
- Warmest regards,
- Sincerely—
- Best,

When emailing people outside of North America, show respect for their more conservative and more respectful approach to business. Use:

- Respectfully
- Respectfully yours

It's always a smart choice, when responding to a customer, to use the same close he used in his email to you. If that seems awkward, select a close that seems one step friendlier. Be careful not to go overboard with your friendliness (xxoo), however.

MIND YOUR EMAIL MANNERS

Recently, I received an email sent from a BlackBerry user. In the fifteen-word message, the writer had two misspellings, used no capitalization, and didn't concern herself with punctuation. The message was followed with this disclaimer: "Sent from my BlackBerry and not spell checked."

What is the behind *that* message? Clearly, she indicated that her time is too valuable to be bothered to spell-check, so gentle reader, deal with it! You, of course, want to convey just the opposite to your buyers.

Show your reader you respect his time by taking your time to pay attention to the details. Unless your response is so urgent that every second counts, be polite! It doesn't cost you anything except an extra moment or two, and the results can be amazing.

Turn your BlackBerry and iPhone's marketing message off. The manufacturers set their marketing message as a default, hopeful that you will let others know you are using their product to communicate. It shouldn't matter to your buyer whether you're communicating from a laptop, a personal device, or a phone. In all instances, stick to standards of proper business communication—and stop marketing for someone other than yourself! Make *how* you're communicating unimportant.

Use Standard Punctuation and Grammar

Always remember that the email you send to your client can be forwarded to his entire organization (on purpose or not) and to your entire organization (on purpose or not). It doesn't matter if you and he are forever friends or drinking buddies. In fact, because you're friends, he may *not even think* that it may reflect poorly on you and your company when he forwards the email you ended with CU L8TR B4N! to the executive committee making the decision on the purchase of the equipment you sell.

Use proper punctuation and grammar to make it easier for your reader to grasp your message. The more quickly and efficiently she can read it, the more likely it is that you'll get the result you want.

Pay Attention to Upper and Lowercase

The best reason to use upper and lowercase properly is this: Your customer can read it more easily and get your point more quickly. Our eyes are accustomed to reading upper and lowercase patterns. In fact, when an all uppercase font is used, we read almost thirteen percent more slowly. Your prospects don't have time to waste. Help them to efficiently decipher your message.

Spell-Check and Reread Every Email You Send

Be certain you correctly spell the words you intend to use. Way too often, I see the incorrect word, correctly spelled. These writers spell-checked but didn't bother to reread after doing so:

Dear Boob (instead of Dear Bob)
Hell, Sue (instead of Hello, Sue)
Will you need a room for your rabbit [rabbi] or will he leave directly following the ceremony?

"Thank you for giving us this opportunity to hose [host]
   your group."
Each manager is responsible for keeping his or her pu-
   bic [public!] area clean.
I'm sorry about the incontinence [inconvenience] I may
   have caused you.

Take the time to reread to ensure you don't mortify
yourself! Let your reader know that details matter to you.

Eliminate Chat Room Speak

As tempting as it may be to use chatty acronyms, don't. It's
like wearing a T-shirt and cargo shorts when you should be
dressed in a collared shirt and nice khakis. Even when
sending business-related IMs (instant messages), be careful
about incorporating chat room terms. Your buyer may not
know what the acronym is supposed to mean and may either discount it, or define it differently than you had
hoped! Instead of saving time, time is wasted when she has
to email you back with "What does 'ATM' mean?" [at this
moment].

Email is the most used sales tool today. Use it to communicate respectfully, honestly, and clearly with your buyer.
Break through the clutter by maintaining a customer-centric
view in everything—from your subject line to the manner in
which you sign off. Separate yourself from the competition
by paying attention to the details. Help your buyer decide
that you are the type of individual he would like to do business with.

Conclusion

I started selling at six years old. My dad, a printer, had an overrun of bumper stickers that his customer didn't need. I can't remember if it was my brother's idea or my own, but we sold those bumper stickers door-to-door for fifteen cents each, or three for a quarter, and everyone in the neighborhood was wise enough to buy three! We were rich beyond our wildest dreams!

A few years later, my mom had me selling (again door-to-door) raffle tickets for the women's organization to which she belonged. If *she* sold enough tickets, she'd be admitted free to their year-end gala luncheon. I remember knocking on a lot of doors, selling one raffle ticket for $2 or three for $5, to get enough tickets sold for that free lunch! Would the selling skills in this book have helped me back then? I actually think our value pricing was more important!

When I started selling Encyclopedia Britannica door-to-door, however, I realized that I had to think of the customer's needs before trying to make the sale. Against every closing technique I had been taught, I actually talked a buyer out of buying (which coincided with my last day selling encyclopedias). The family was dirt poor and there was a public library less than two blocks away. I just couldn't let them pay off those books for the next twelve years.

Today's sales environment requires even more thought, respect, and love for the customer. The more we can show passion for our customers' success, communicate with them responsively and respectfully, and help them feel safe and smart, the more likely we are to build relationships, boost sales, and beat the competition. I'm hopeful the ideas in this book will help you achieve those goals.

Now that you've finished the first read of this book, please don't put it on the bookshelf! It won't do you any good there. Keep it in your backpack or briefcase and reread the sections you know will help you drive sales, build relationships, and increase revenue. Select one or two strategic concepts to apply, and work only on those, until they become a natural part of your sales conversation. Once you own those strategies, take the book out again, and select two new ones to apply. Use what you've learned to bring success to others and create even greater success for yourself.

About the Author

Photo by Jeff Newton

Sue Hershkowitz-Coore (sue@speakersue.com) is an internationally recognized sales trainer and speaker. As the founder and CEO of High Impact Presentation Skills, Sue has presented sales strategies and success principles to over 2 million people in forty-nine states and seven international venues. She is also the author of *Power Sales Writing* (McGraw-Hill). Sue's client list includes some of the most prestigious and forward-thinking sales organizations in the global marketplace. She has been named a "Platinum" speaker for six consecutive years by the prestigious 20,500-member Meeting Professionals International. Sue lives in Scottsdale, Arizona, with her husband, Bill.

How to Contact the Author

For further information or to schedule
Sue Hershkowitz-Coore to speak to your group,
please contact
High Impact Presentations at 480-575-9711
or visit
www.speakersue.com

Also Available in the How to Say It® Series...

How to Say It® at Work, Revised: Power Words, Phrases, Body Language, and Communication Secrets for Getting Ahead by Jack Griffin (October 2008)

How to Say It®: Marketing with New Media: A Guide to Promoting Your Small Business Using Websites, E-zines, Blogs, and Podcasts by Lena Claxton and Alison Woo (September 2008)

How to Say It®: Business Writing That Works: The Simple, 10-Step Target Outline System to Help You Reach Your Bottom Line by Adina Rishe Gewirtz

How to Say It® to Get into the College of Your Choice: Application, Essay, and Interview Strategies to Get You the Big Envelope by Linda Metcalf

How to Say It® for Executives: The Complete Guide to Communication for Leaders by Phyllis Mindell

How to Say It® to Seniors: Closing the Communication Gap with Our Elders by David Solie

How to Say It® When You Don't Know What to Say: The Right Words For Difficult Times by Robbie Miller Kaplan

How to Say It® for Women: Communicating with Confidence and Power Using the Language of Success by Phyllis Mindell

How to Say It® to Teens: Talking About the Most Important Topics of Their Lives by Richard Heyman

How to Say It® to Your Kids: The Right Words to Solve Problems, Soothe Feelings & Teach Values by Dr. Paul Coleman

How to Say It® with Your Voice by Jeffrey Jacobi

How to Say It® Pocket Guides

How to Say It®: Negotiating to Win by Jim Hennig, PhD (August 2008)

How to Say It® to Sell It: Key Words, Phrases, and Strategies to Build Relationships, Boost Revenue, and Beat the Competition by Sue Hershkowitz-Coore

How to Say It®: Job Interviews by Linda Matias

How to Say It®: Performance Reviews: Phrases and Strategies for Painless and Productive Performance Reviews by Meryl Runion and Janelle Brittain

How to Say It®: Persuasive Presentations by Jeffrey Jacobi